# COLOR ME BLAKE!

## An Adult Coloring Book

### based on the psychedelic art of a Romantic poet

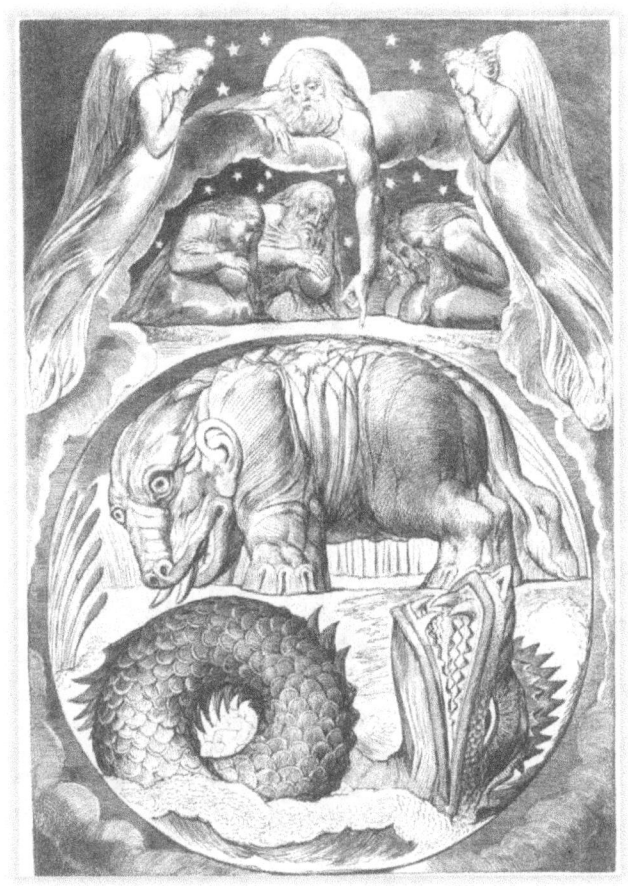

A coloring book experience created by Jacki Price.

Cover by Jacki Price.
Copyright © 2019 by Jacquelynn Price-Linnartz.  All rights reserved.
ISBN: 9781795581035

# PRACTICE PAGE

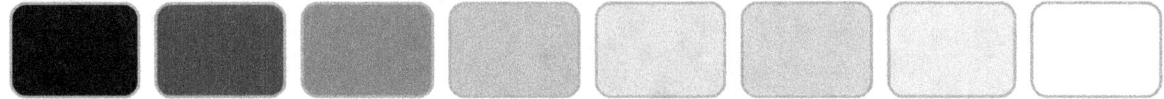

Test your coloring tools here.

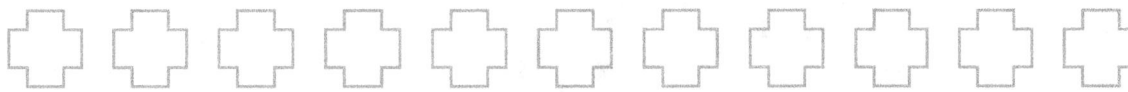

Try out your implements and color options here to check for color, bleed, saturation, and size of your tools' marks.

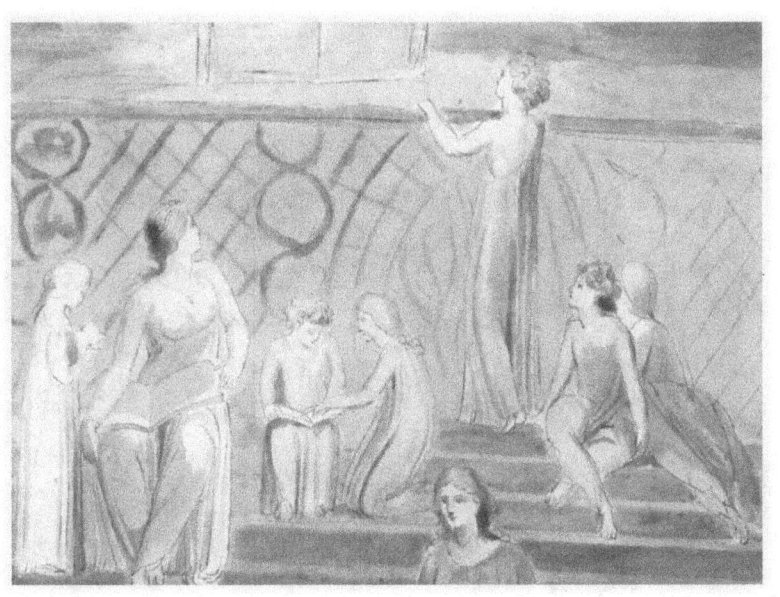

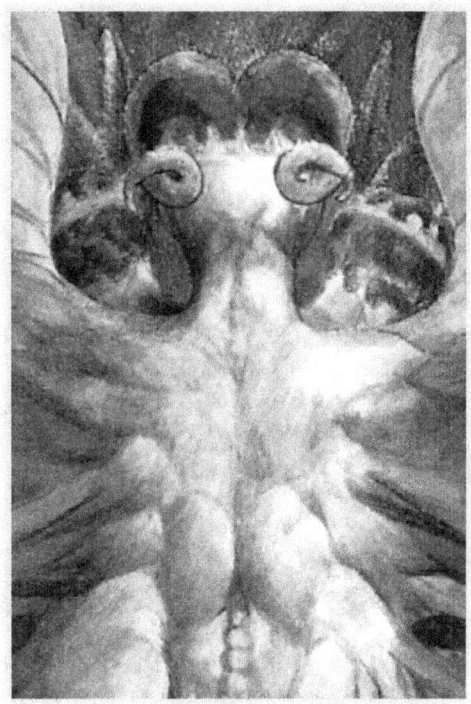

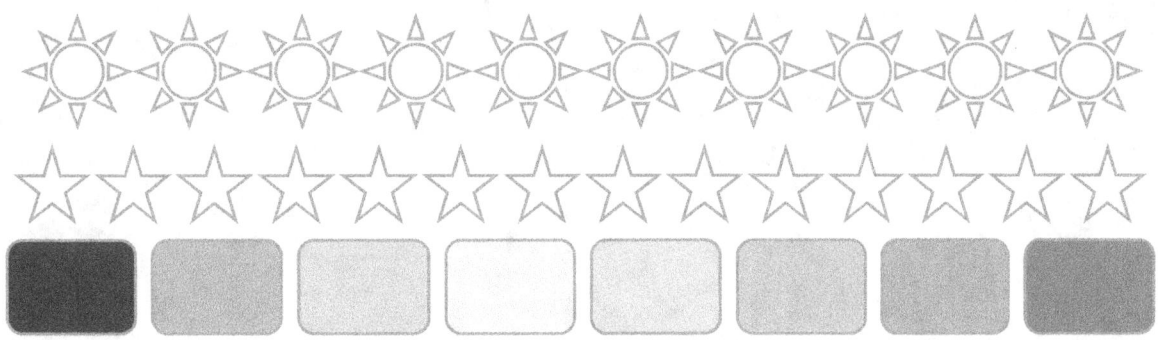

# WELCOME, COLORIST!

- I've included two of each coloring page in case you'd like to test out different coloring ideas or if you'd like to share.

- To reduce bleed-through, each image gets its own sheet.

- You'll find potentially boring facts about the images, and maybe some quotes, before each coloring page.

# COLORING TIPS

- Use a loose sheet of paper, paperboard, or posterboard under your current page.

- These pages do NOT tear out—trust me, I've tried! Craft knives and scissors work better.

- Trying coloring dark and gray areas!  I did the cover with pencils.

- If something seems too small to color, don't worry.  The Blakes blended colors across the lines all the time.  It's artistic 😉

- If you make a mistake, don't sweat it!  You can incorporate it into a new color scheme for your work, and there are two of each image if you'd like to start over.

- When you like the finished work, claim it and frame it!  Post its photo on *Color Me Blake*'s Amazon product page as a "customer image"—we'd all love to see it!

# A word from your author:
# WHO WAS THIS WILLIAM BLAKE FELLOW?

How to describe Blake ‑‑

Blake was a man who was born, who lived, and who later died.

Blake was a man who had a job, and a wife, and some children.

And Blake was a man who happened to see visions that inspired an intense, mind-boggling belief system expressed in intense, mind-boggling art.

William Blake (1757–1827) was a British Romantic artist and poet whose work influenced the likes of Dante Gabrielle Rosetti, William Butler Yeats, Allen Ginsberg, Aldous Huxley, Benjamin Britten, Bob Dylan, Jim Morrison, Van Morrison, and many other artsy types. His most famous writings—which he illustrated—include Songs of Innocence and Experience, The Book of Thel, The Marriage of Heaven and Hell, and Jerusalem. He illustrated works like the Book of Job, John Milton's Paradise Lost, John Bunyan's Pilgrim's Progress, and Dante Alighieri's Divine Comedy. Some say he was a devoted husband whose wife colored some of his illustrations. Well done, Blake, well done.

This collection of his art shows just how much Blake was influenced by the Christian scriptures and Western "classicism," although his religious beliefs weren't exactly traditional or mainstream. Scholars argue about his beliefs and the complex mythical system he devised as he aged. All debate aside, though, his art is nothing if not bursting with fantastical imagination. This guy makes pious art seem downright trippy.

I've adapted a choice selection of Blake's art, making it ready for you to color with your unique creative vision. The collection here samples works from a variety of Blake's endeavors, altered just enough for you to make your mark. Experiment, have fun, and, when you like the result, hang it on a wall with pride (and post a photo on our Amazon page!).

With this coloring book, let Blake's creativity spark your own. Pick up where he left off. Take hold of the old and make something new.

Let your imagination soar!

# SCRAP PAGE

If you don't have something better, then you can rip out this page to use as a separator between your pages as you color. That will help protect the lower pages.

And because there's so much space here, let's have some acknowledgements!

Special thanks to the Athenaeum and its contributors for their efforts in sharing the artwork of William Blake and making that art available to the wider world.

Thanks also to all Blake scholars and those museums and galleries and archives who have dedicated countless hours to bringing the psychedelic imagination of William Blake into the 21$^{st}$ century.

And thank you, the colorist, without whom this coloring book doesn't make a lick of sense.

Thank you thank you thank you.

Okay. There's still more space here. So, on the back, you'll find a list of ways you can learn more about William Blake! Yippie.

# Learn More about Blake

## (A.k.a., a Bibliography of Bibliographies & Archives)

## The William Blake Archive.

http://www.blakearchive.org

This is *the* place for all things Blake.   Seriously, it's amazing.

## Stephen C. Behrendt's bibliography.

### Currently living at

http://english.unl.edu/sbehrendt/courses/931Blake/BibFall2005.htm

## The Athenaeum: http://www.the-athenaeum.org/

## The Tate: https://www.tate.org.uk/

# PART 1

# SAMPLING BLAKE'S IDEOLOGY

# AGE TEACHING YOUTH

c. 1785-1790
Ink & watercolor on paper.
10.8 cm X 8 cm.
Location: Tate Britain.

According to the Tate, the three figures might represent the law (the old man), nature and its imitation (the young person drawing), and imagination (the girl reaching toward the skies).

If that's the case, then Blake probably didn't think that "age teaching youth" was all that great. He advocated a balance of these traits, and he thought his society was way out of whack by over-privileging old-man law.

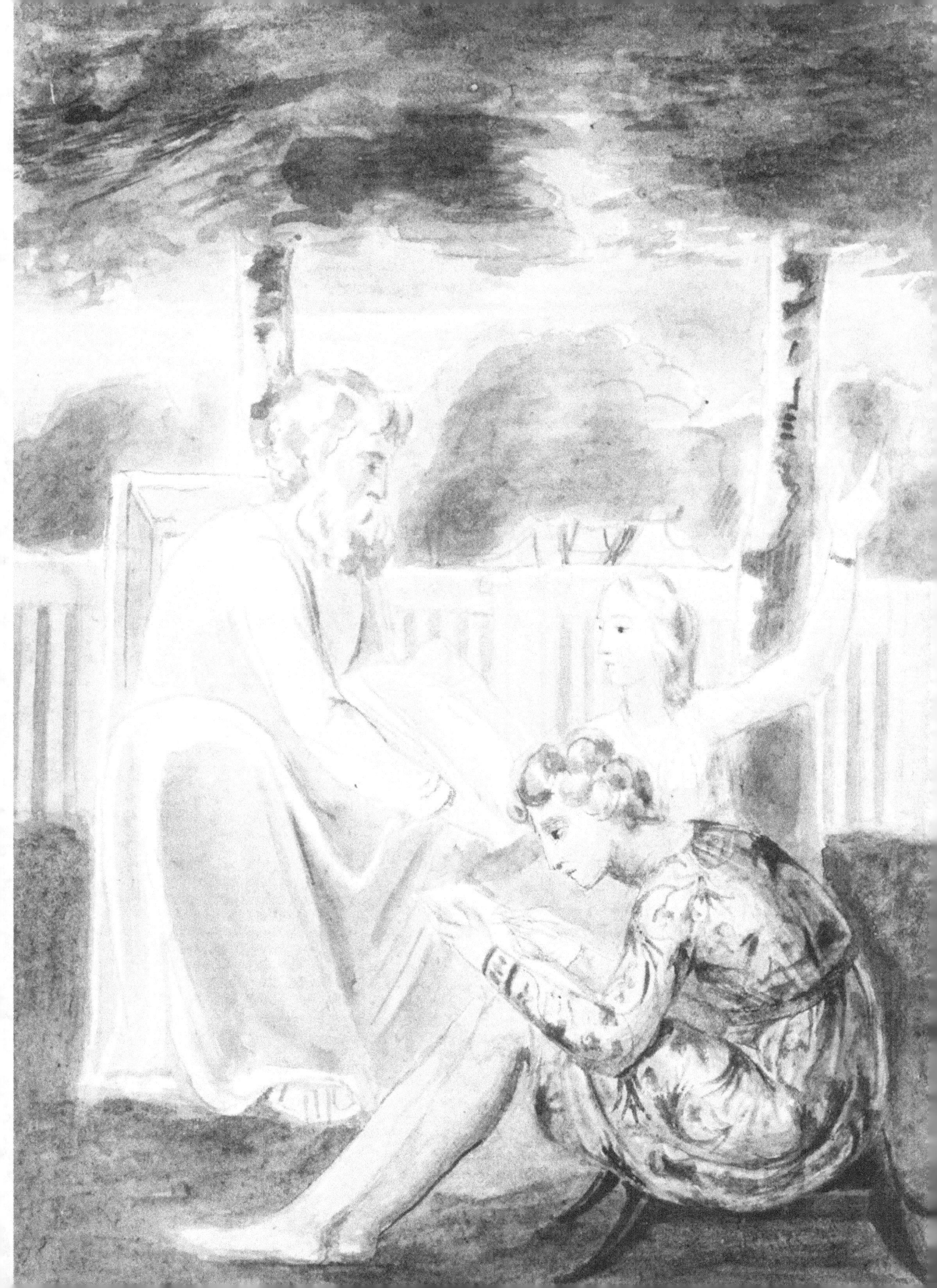

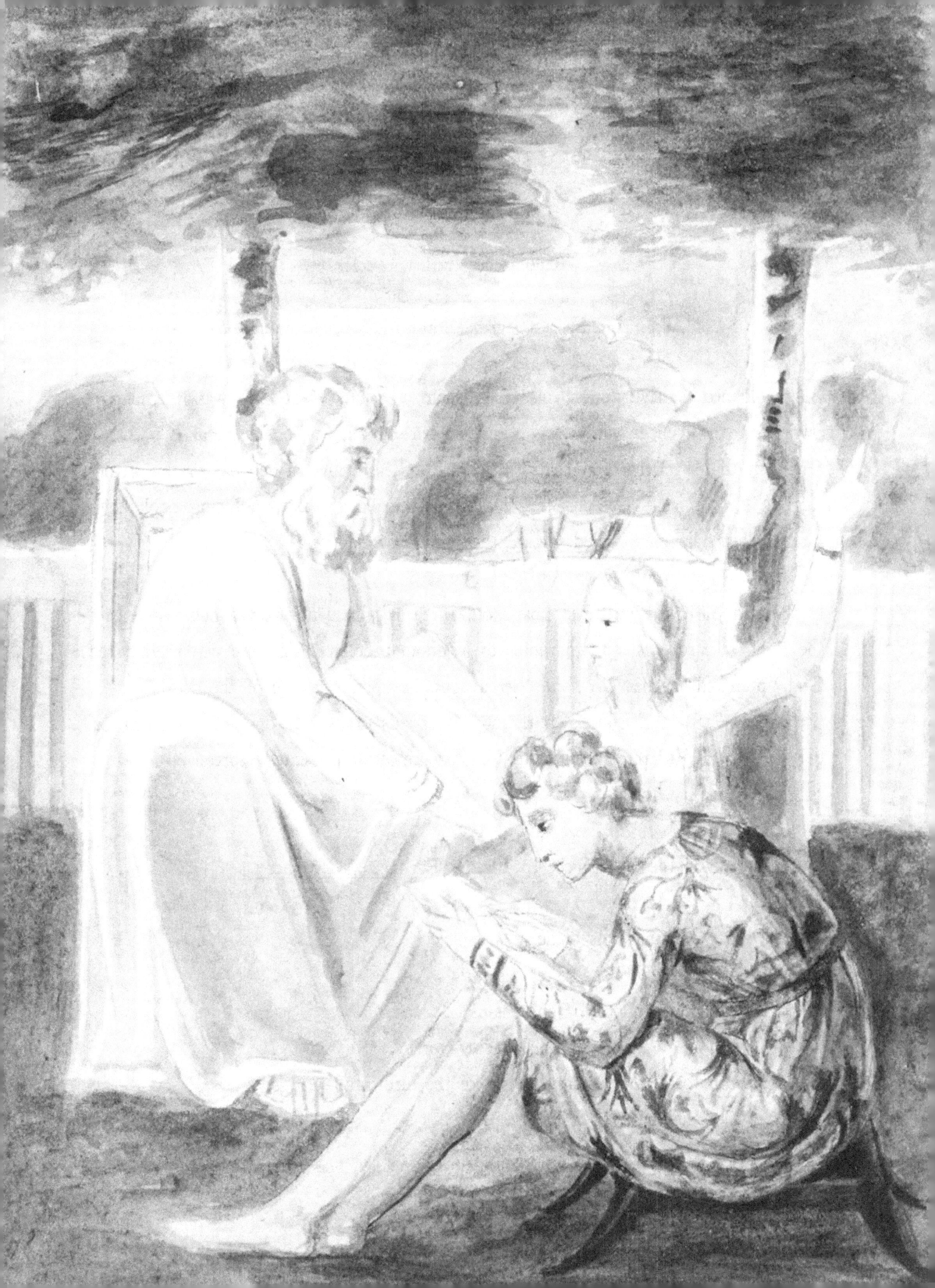

# ANCIENT OF DAYS

c. 1794
Relief etching with watercolor.
16.8 x 23.3 cm.
Locations: Library of Congress, British Museum, and several others.

Blake claimed to have gotten this image from a vision. Not only was it among his favorites to reproduce, but it was a fast favorite among his contemporaries. A testament to its relative popularity, there are at least thirteen versions of it. Still running strong, you'll see this image all over the place today, including book covers like Stephen Hawking's God Created the Integers and the this one 😊

It shows a biblically informed image of a creator—Urizen—with a compass. In the Book of Proverbs, the character of Wisdom proclaims that she was there when God "prepared the heavens" and "set a compass upon the face of the depth" (Proverbs 27:8). In Blake's mythology, Urizen's exact role or symbolism evolved, but, a zing to Enlightenment values, Urizen always represented repressive reason/rationality.

This image was the frontispiece of Blake's Europe: A Prophecy.

'Again the night is come,
That strong Urthona takes his rest;
And Urizen, unloos'd from chains,
Glows like a meteor in the distant North.
Stretch forth your hands and strike the elemental strings!
Awake the thunders of the deep!

- Europe: A Prophecy, lines 9-14

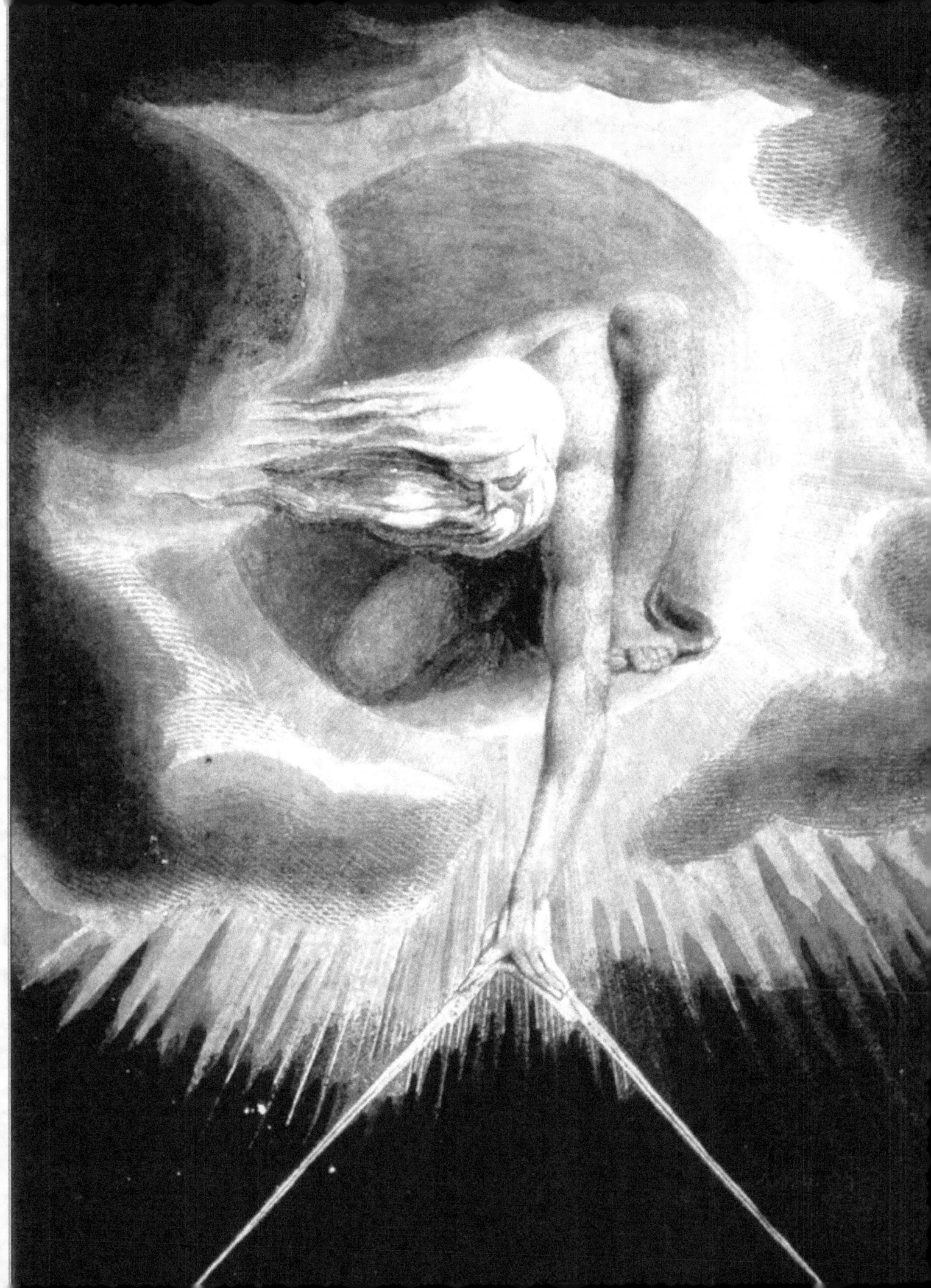

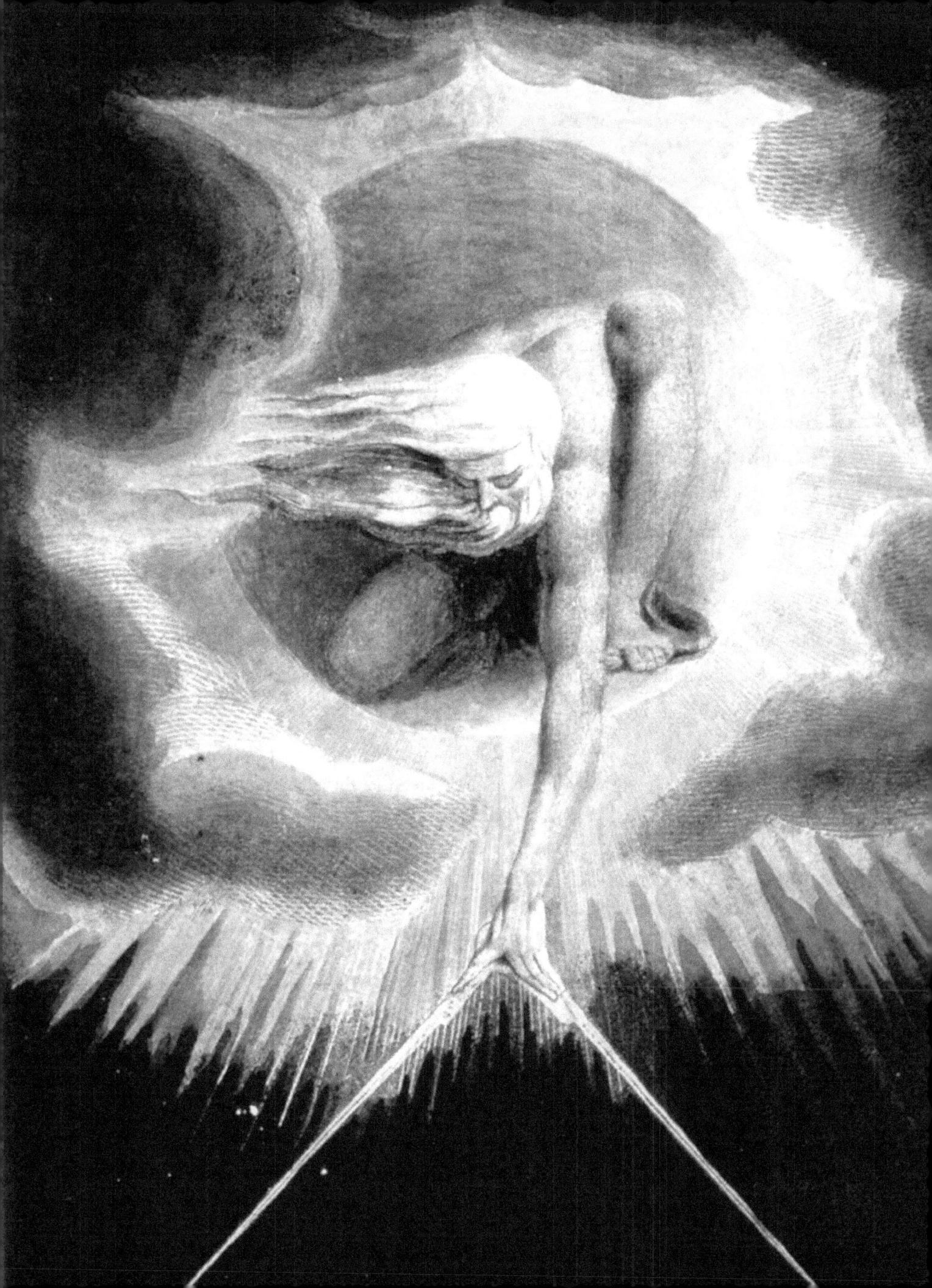

# AN ALLEGORY OF THE BIBLE

c. 1780-1785
Graphite, ink, & watercolor on paper.
61.5 x 34.9 cm.
Locations: Library of Congress, Tate Britain, several others.

How is this an allegory of the Bible?  In the picture, a book reveals something to enlighten some people.  Other than that, who knows?

This huge watercolor, an early work of Blake's, does not yet have an accepted description among his groupies (a.k.a. "Blake scholars").  Some have wondered if it illustrates the Christian journey, as with his illustrations for Pilgrim's Progress, although it would've been incredibly early for that specific project.  Others say it shows the revelation of knowledge through the Bible, which would fit with Blake's worldview in which the Bible reveals truth despite his disenchantment with established religion.

Blake makes clear that his vision of Christ and the Bible sharply contrasts with that of his contemporaries in his "The Everlasting Gospel," lines 1-9:

> The Vision of Christ that thou dost see
> Is my vision's greatest enemy.
> Thine is the Friend of all Mankind;
> Mine speaks in parables to the blind.
> Thine loves the same world that mine hates;
> Thy heaven doors are my hell gates.
> Socrates taught what Meletus
> Loath'd as a nation's bitterest curse,
> And Caiaphas was in his own mind
> A benefactor to mankind.
> Both read the Bible day and night,
> But thou read'st black where I read white.

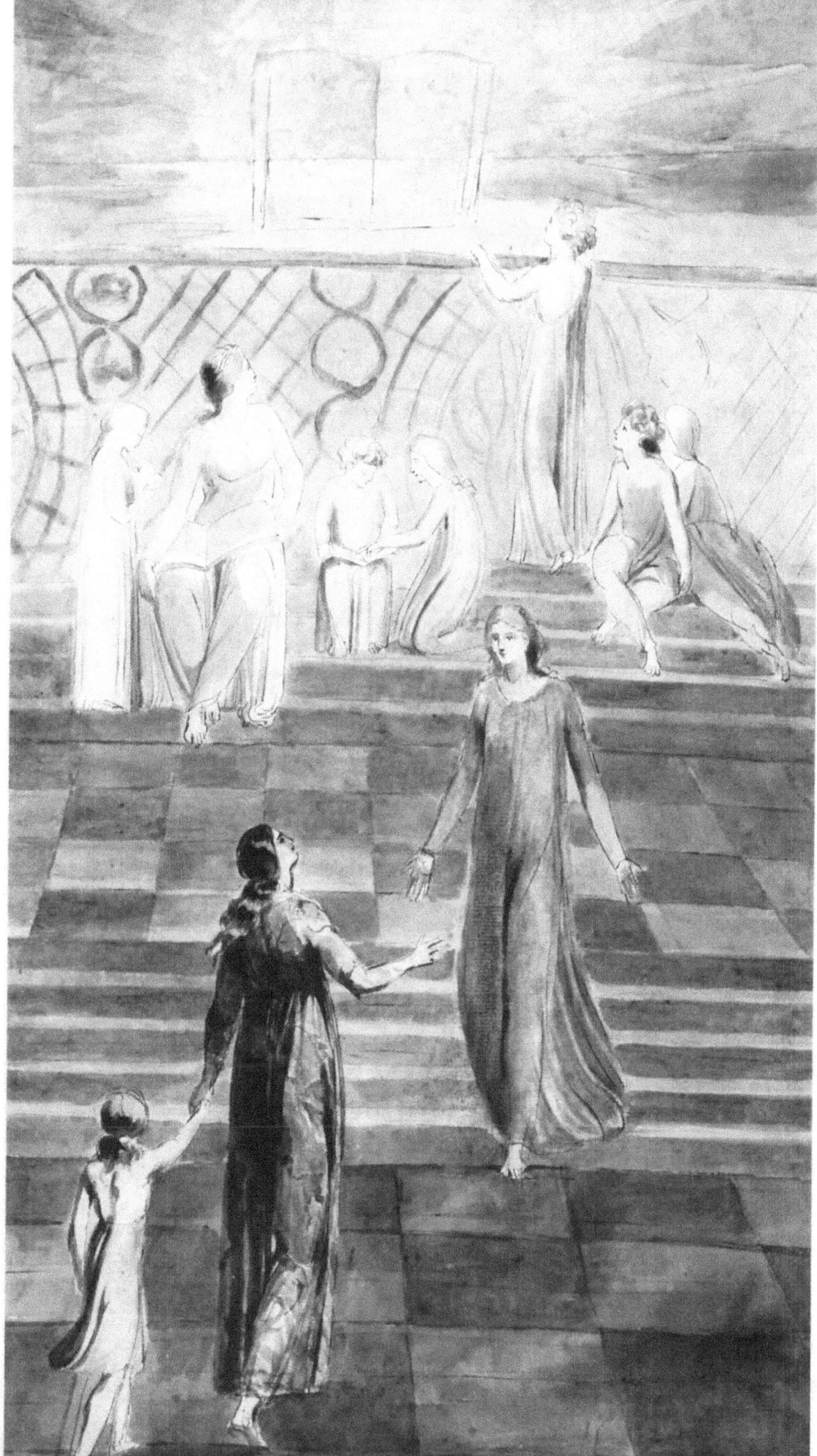

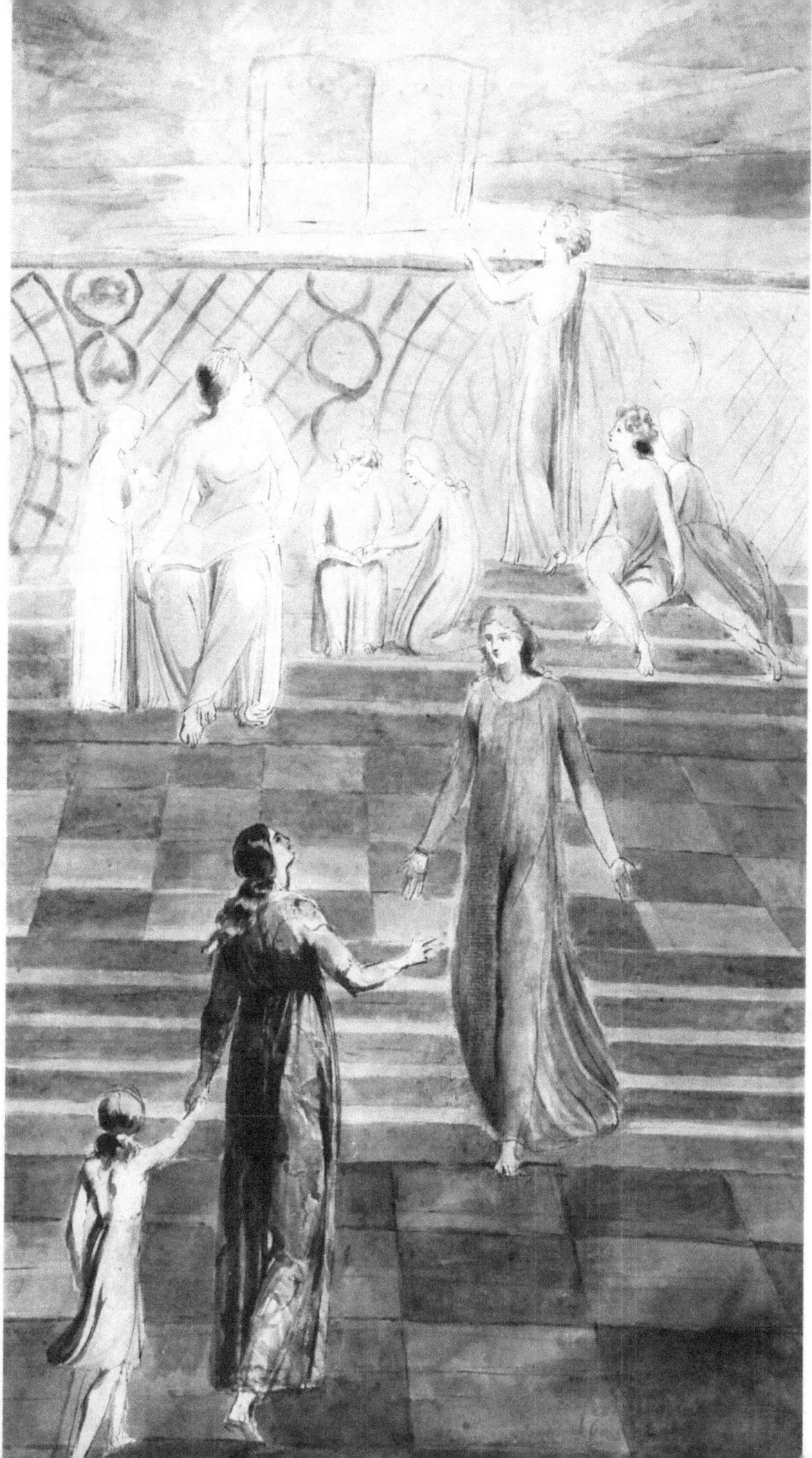

# PART 2

# OLD TESTAMENT / HEBREW BIBLE THEMES

# ELOHIM CREATING ADAM

c. 1795-1805
Color print, ink, & watercolor on paper.
43.1 x 53.6 cm.
Location: Tate Britain.

Factoid:

> The creation story of Genesis 1 uses "Elohim" to refer to God in the original Hebrew.
>
> The creation story of Genesis 2 uses "LORD God" (the usual English translation for *YHWH*) instead.

The title of Blake's image here combines the "Elohim" of Gen. 1 with the story of Gen. 2.

Genesis 2:7 - "Then the LORD God created the human [*Adam*, or *ha'adam*] out of the dirt of the ground [*adamah*]…"

"Elohim Creating Adam" shows both Blake's love of scripture and his own unique mythology. On the one hand, this image shows the moment when God ("Elohim") creates "Adam," the first human, illustrating an account in the Book of Genesis. On the other hand, according to the Tate, Blake believed that humanity "fell" when it was taken from the spiritual realm and put in the physical, material realm by way of this same act of creation. Geez, Blake, that's a real bummer.

"With sharp pangs...brought forth an infant form / where was a worm before. … The Eternals their tent finished / alarm'd with these gloomy visions / when Enitharmon groaning / produc'd a man Child to the light." –Urizen, 6.6-7

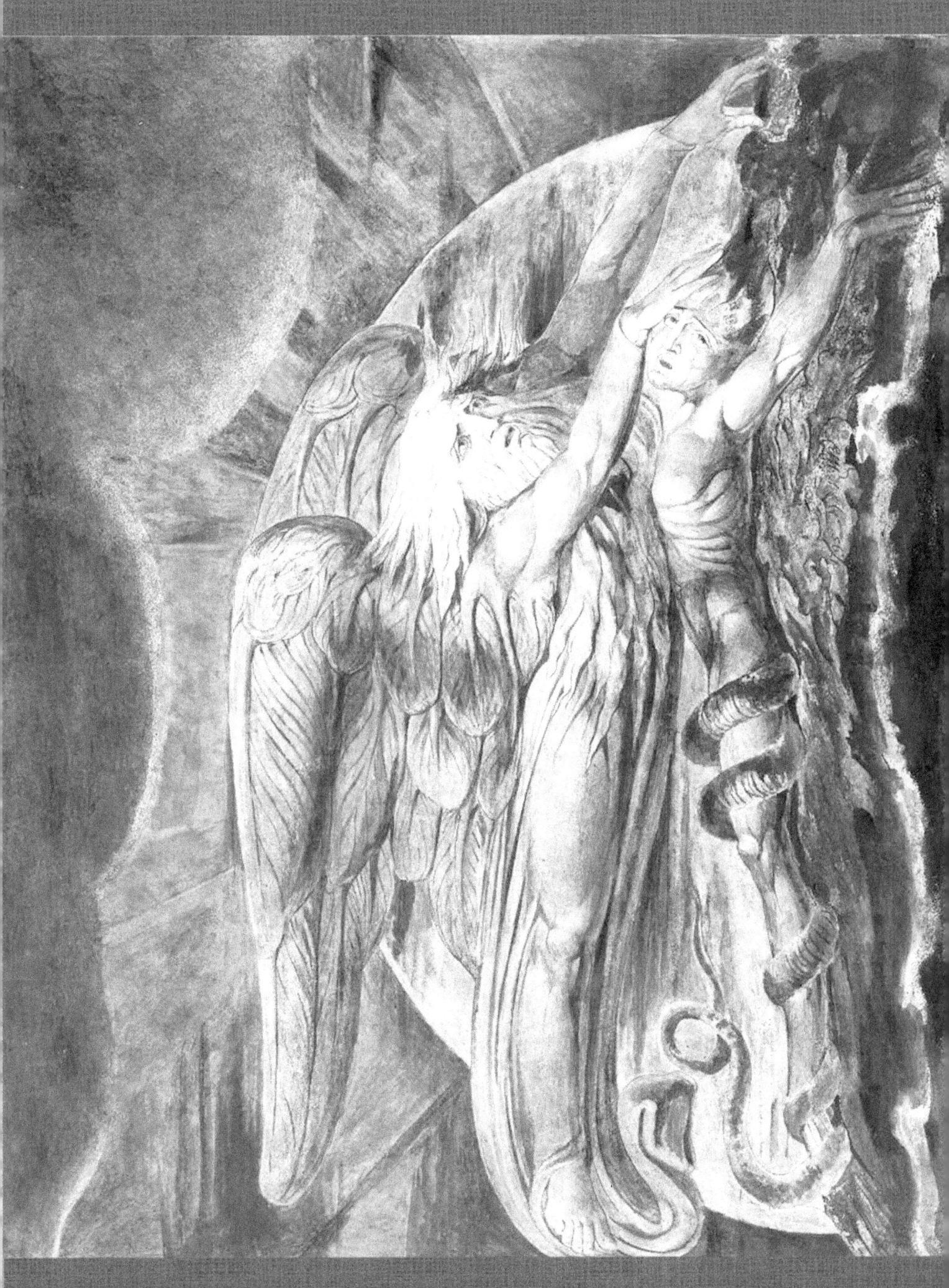

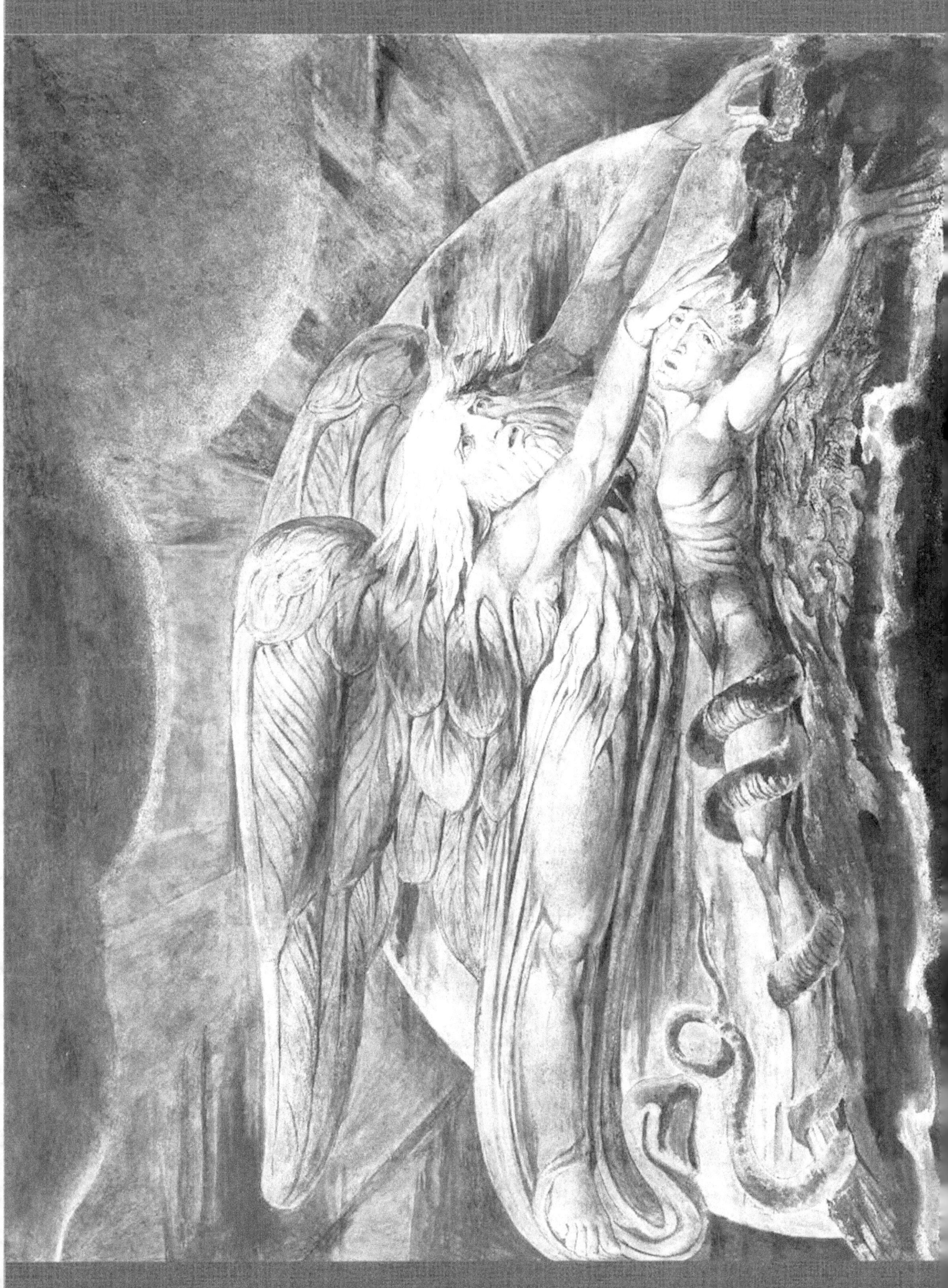

# THE BODY OF ABEL
# FOUND BY ADAM AND EVE

c. 1826

Ink, tempera, and gold on mahogany.

32.5 x 43.3 cm.

Location: Tate Britain.

I'll be honest, friends—the first time I saw this, I had *no* idea what kind of disturbing nonsense I was looking at.   Until I read the title.

Here, Blake imagines a poignant moment of the Genesis 4 story of Cain and Abel. In the story, the jealous Cain takes sibling rivalry to the up-teenth level by murdering his brother Abel.   Blake brings the emotional side of the story to life by showing the parents' grief and Cain's shame in what amounts to a pretty horrific scene.

Eve:     Is this the Promise of Jehovah?   O! it is all a vain delusion
                This Death, and this Life, and this Jehovah!
Jehovah: Woman, lift thine eyes!

                                    —Blake's The Ghost of Abel, lines 13-15.

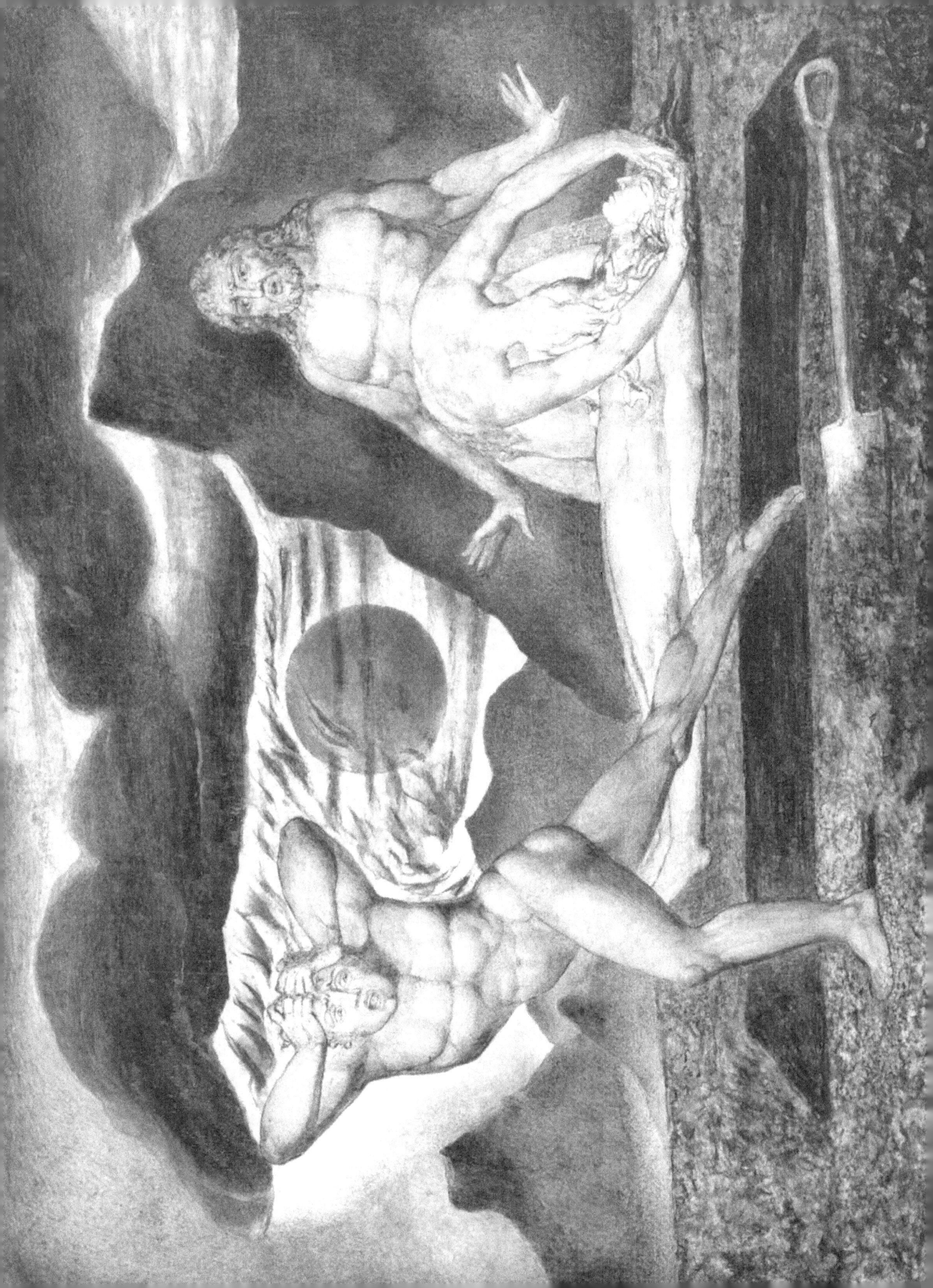

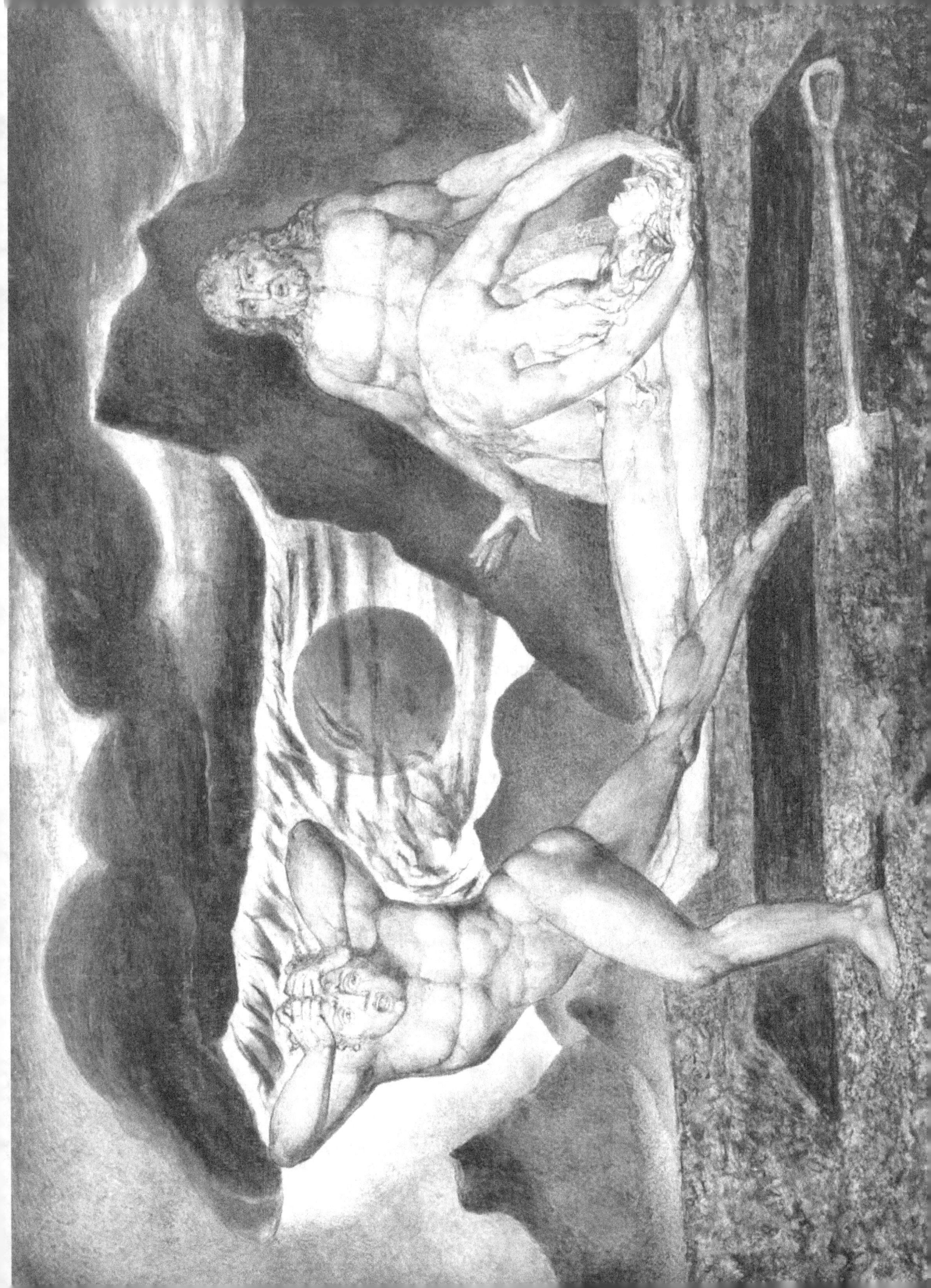

# BEHEMOTH AND LEVIATHAN

1825, reprinted 1874
Line engraving on paper.
Location: Tate Britain, with other versions elsewhere, e.g. the Morgan Library & Museum.

In the margins, Blake quotes from the Book of Job: Job 36:29, 40:19, 41:34, 37:11, and 40:15.

This image has a lot going on. One of his illustrations for the Book of Job, it shows that part of the story when God gives Job the what-for by describing how God created these crazy-awesome creatures, the Leviathan and Behemoth, who respectively rule the land and sea. God basically says, "Try doing *that*, Job, then get back to me." Knowing Blake, though, it's no surprise that scholars suspect several layers of symbolism going on here, like warfare and Admiral Lord Nelson and something pessimistic about material existence.

Leviathan and Behemoth,

    ‑‑the War by Sea enormous & the War

    By Land astounding; erecting pillars in the deepest Hell

    to reach the heavenly arches.

                    –Blake's <u>Jerusalem</u>, 91:39-42.

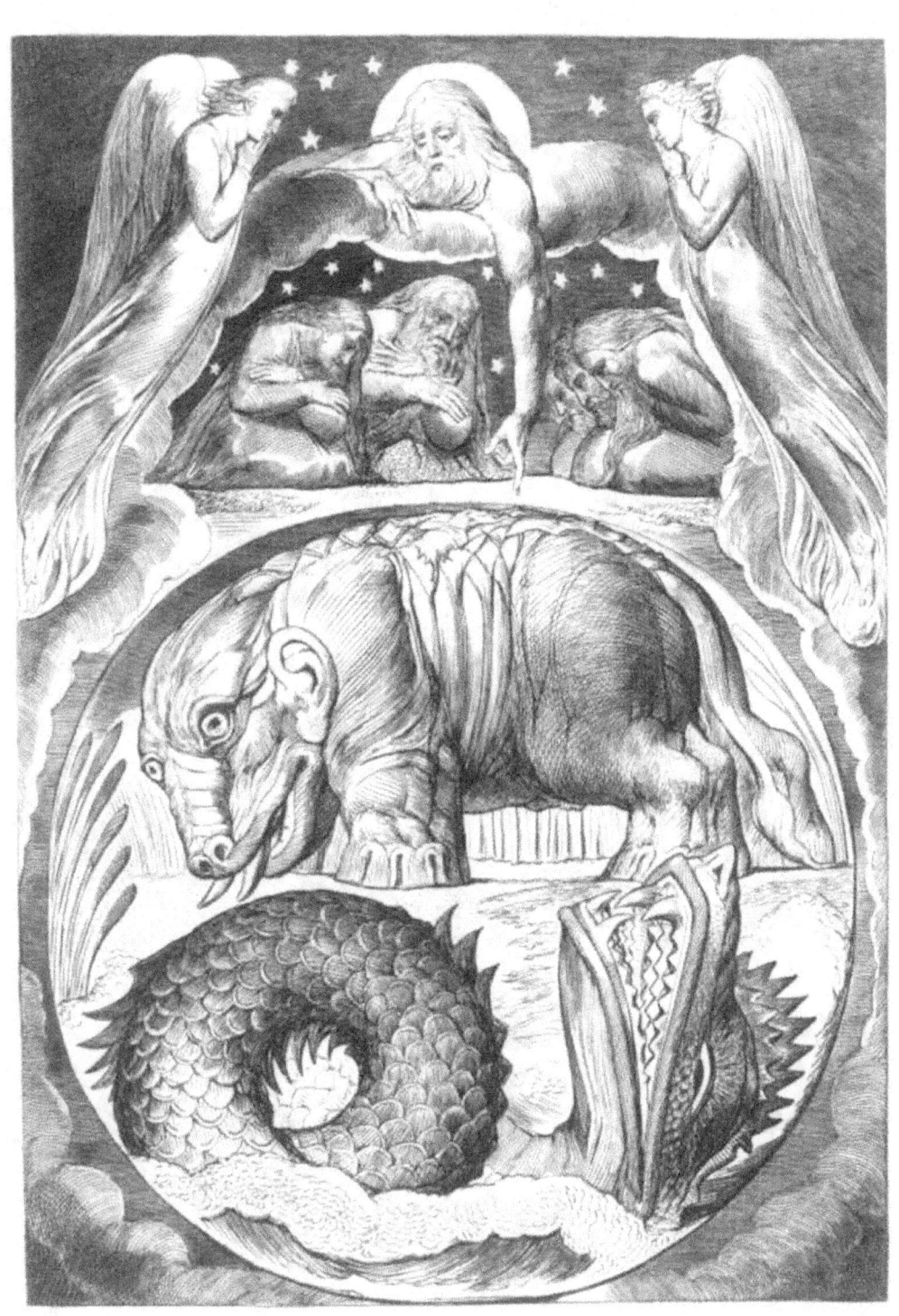

Can any understand the spreadings of the Clouds
the noise of his Tabernacle

Also by watering he wearieth the thick cloud by his counsels
He scattereth the bright cloud also it is turned about

Of Behemoth he saith He is the chief of the ways of God
Of Leviathan he saith He is King over all the Children of Pride

Behold now Behemoth which I made with thee

Can any understand the spreadings of the Clouds
the noise of his Tabernacle

Also by watering he wearieth the thick cloud
He scattereth the bright cloud also it is turned about by his counsels

Of Behemoth he saith He is the chief of the ways of God
Of Leviathan he saith, He is King over all the Children of Pride

Behold now Behemoth which I made with thee

# DAVID DELIVERED OUT OF MANY WATERS

c. 1805
Ink & watercolor on paper.
41.5 x 34.8 cm.
Location: Tate Britain.

In this super-Christian interpretation of Psalm 18, Jesus (in the role of the Psalm's LORD God) descends through the heavens on cherubim, glowing with self-generated light, to rescue the ensnared and drowning David. Blake shows seven cherubim even though the Psalm doesn't specify that number, perhaps drawing on the Christian tradition of seven archangels.

Check out these passages from the Psalm to see some of the connections.

3 I will call on the LORD, who is worthy to be praised: so I will be saved from mine enemies.

4 The cords of death encompassed me, and the floods of destruction overwhelmed me.

5 The cords of hell encompassed me: the snares of death trapped me.

6 In my distress I…cried to my God. From his temple, he heard my voice…

9 He bowed the heavens and came down, darkness under his feet.

10 And he rode on a cherub, flying on the wings of the wind.

11 He made darkness his covering, a pavilion of dark rainclouds.

12 Thick clouds moved in the brightness of his presence…

16 …From above, he took me and drew me out of many waters.

17 He delivered me from my strong enemy…

24 Therefore the LORD rewarded me according to my righteousness…

28 [God] will light my candle: the LORD my God will light my darkness.

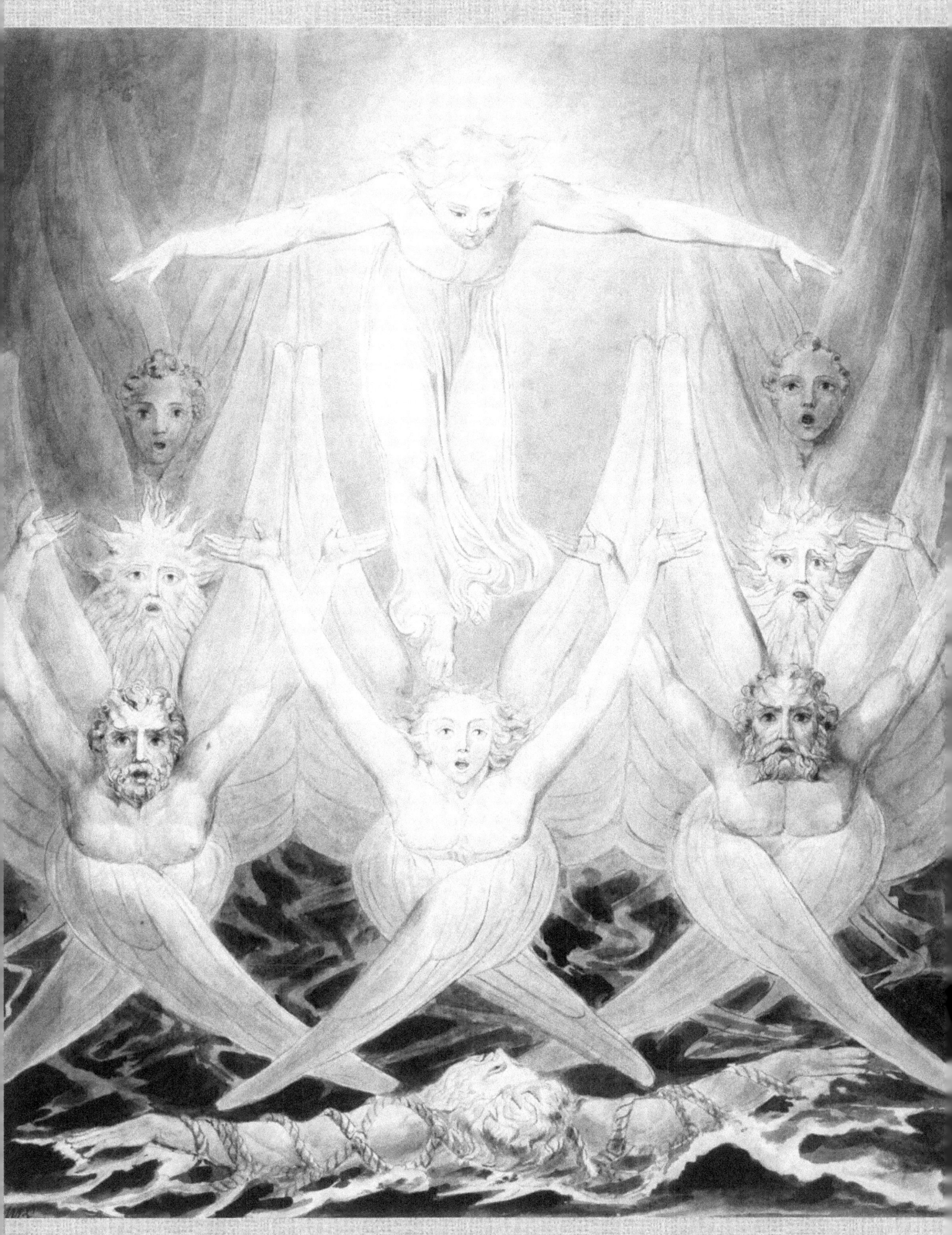

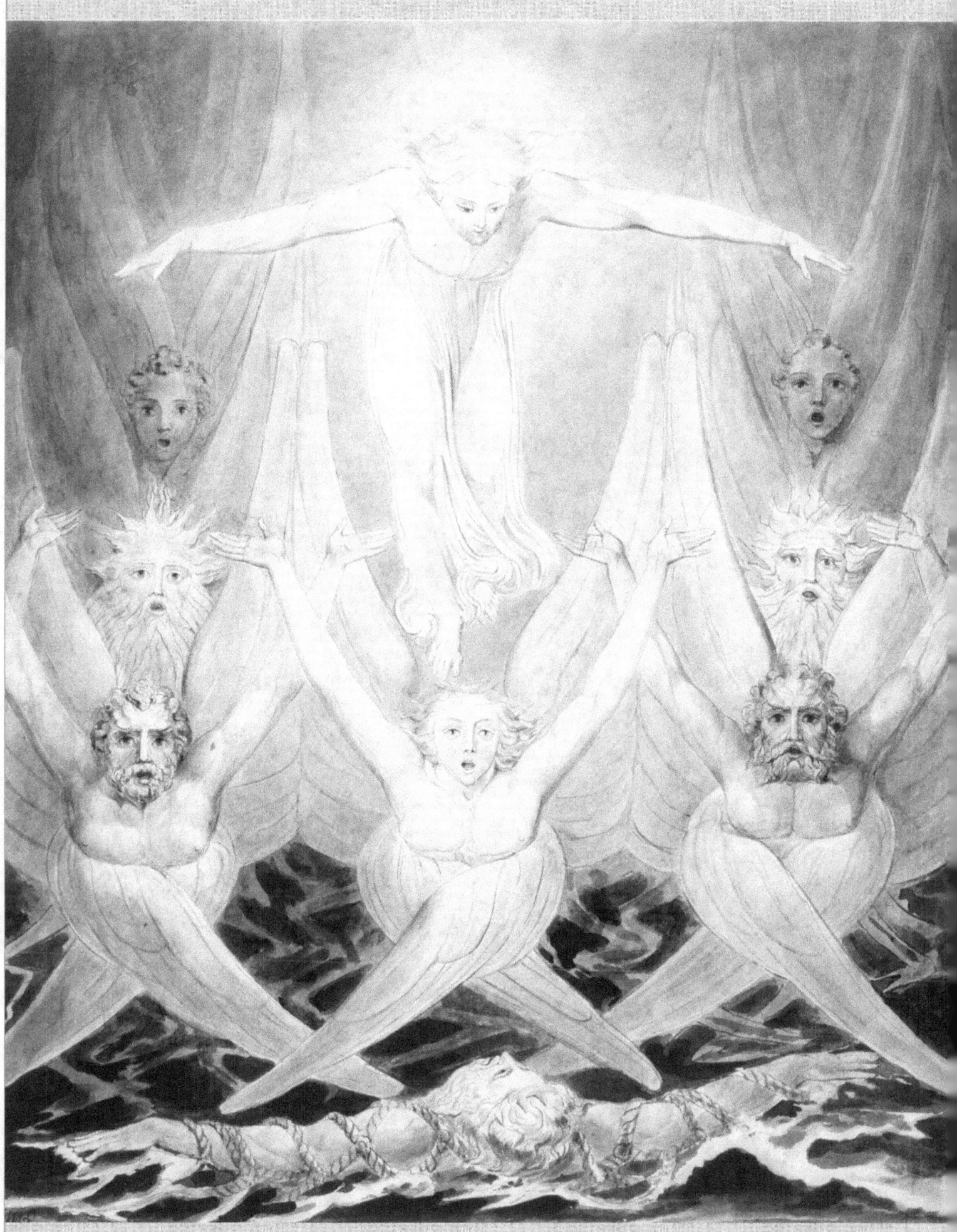

# PART 3

# PASSION & DEATH OF JESUS

# THE AGONY IN THE GARDEN

c. 1799-1800
Tempera on iron.
27 x 38 cm.
Location: Tate Britain.

"The Agony in the Garden" illustrates Luke 22:43-44.

Blake had a thing for agony.

Here, he illustrates a passage specific to the Gospel of Luke's version of Jesus in the Garden of Gethsemane. In the Garden, Jesus contemplates what was about to happen to him—betrayal, arrest, torture, and crucifixion. Very loosely translated, he prays, "Please, Father, don't let this fall to me if we can pull off your plan in any other way. But what you want is more important, and I'll do whatever it takes." He's afraid and desperate.

Luke's account includes a verse that further highlights Jesus's very human fear, distress, and physical agony:

> And there appeared an angel unto him from heaven, strengthening him. And being in agony, he prayed more earnestly: and his sweat was [like] great drops of blood falling down to the ground. (Luke 22:43-44, KJV)

Jesus's posture prefigures his imminent death on the cross. The brilliant glow casts this agony and imminent death in a more hopeful light.

Don't be afraid to color the darkness!
And yes, those are creepers and sleepers in the shadows.

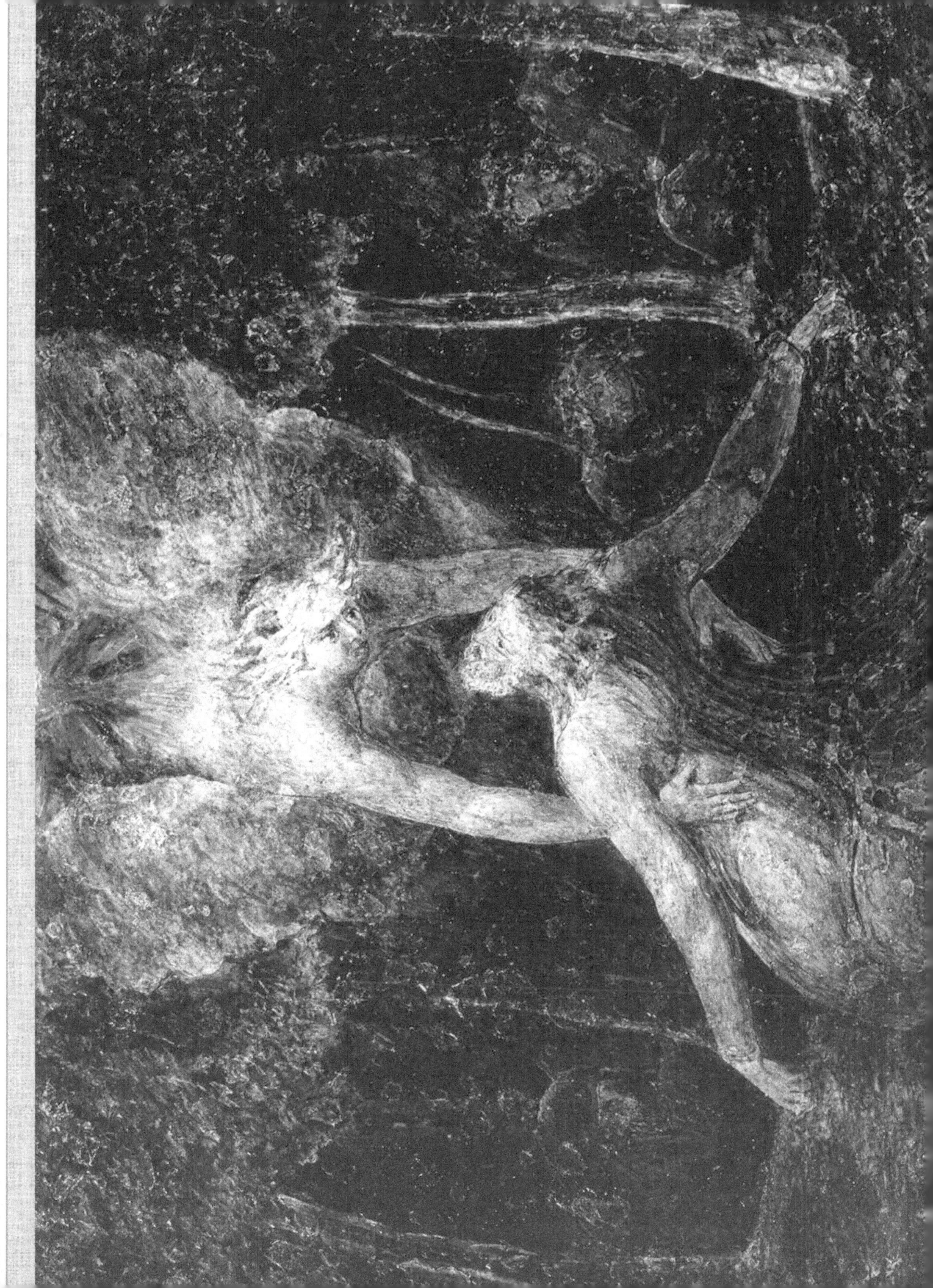

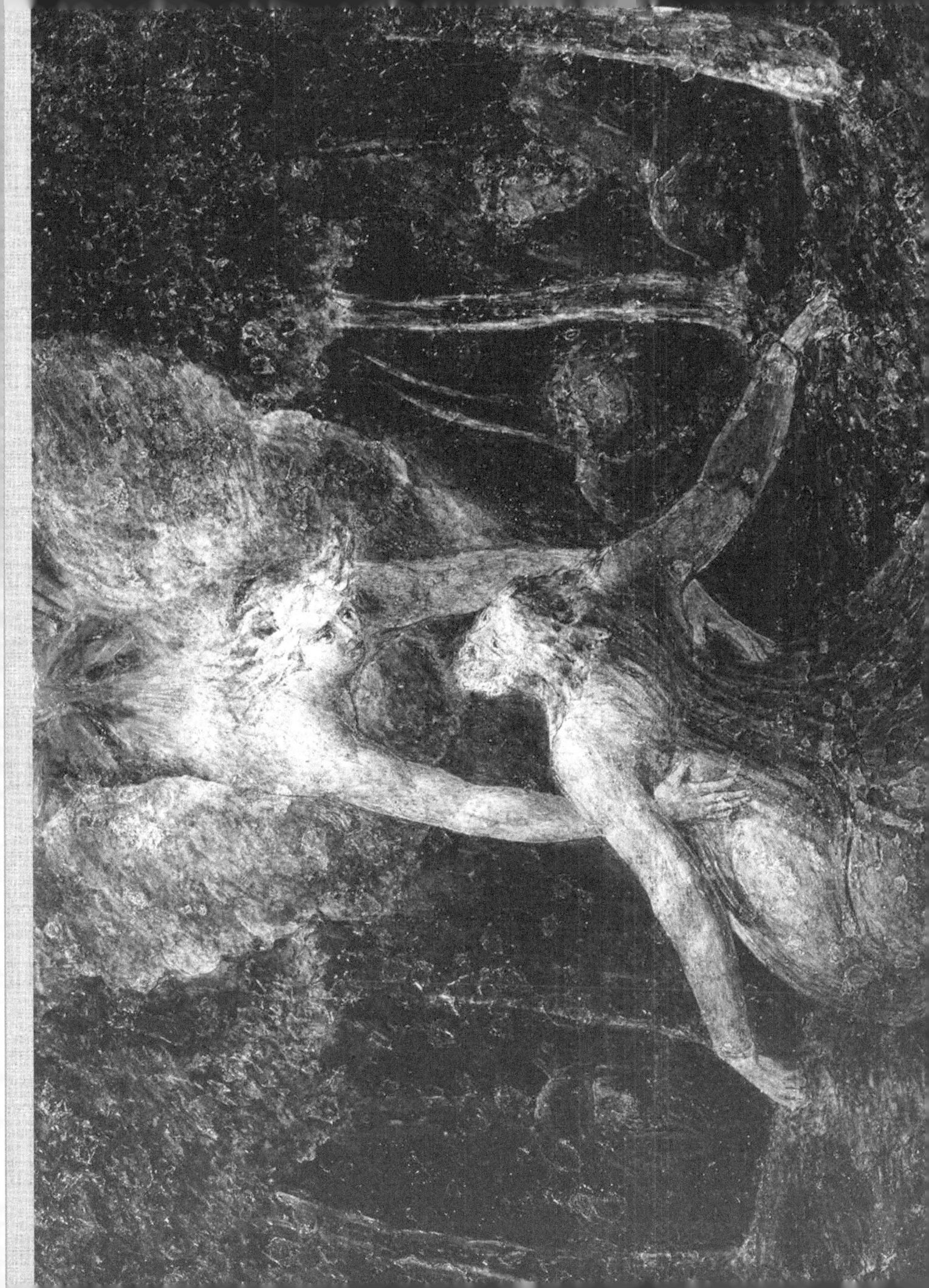

# THE CRUCIFIXION: BEHOLD THY MOTHER

c. 1805
Ink & watercolor on paper.
41.3 x 30 cm.
Location: Tate Britain.

This crucifixion scene illustrates the moment in John 19 when Jesus plays family match-maker with his mother, Mary, and John, one of his disciples.   He tells John to accept Mary as his mother, and Mary to accept John as a son.   This way, they will both get the benefits of such a relationship after Jesus's death.

In the picture, Mary and John bask in the supernatural glow of Jesus, sharing in his revelatory love.   Even with all this love going on, Blake shows this as a very somber moment.   Muted colors with hidden faces and eerie lighting—and a Jesus who seems kind of cool with all of this—help this picture seem pretty darn ghostly.

John 19: 26-27 (King James Version, the version Blake would've read):
> When Jesus therefore saw his mother, and the disciple standing by, whom he loved, he saith unto his mother, 'Woman, behold thy son!'
> Then saith he to the disciple, 'Behold thy mother!'   And from that hour that disciple took her unto his own home.

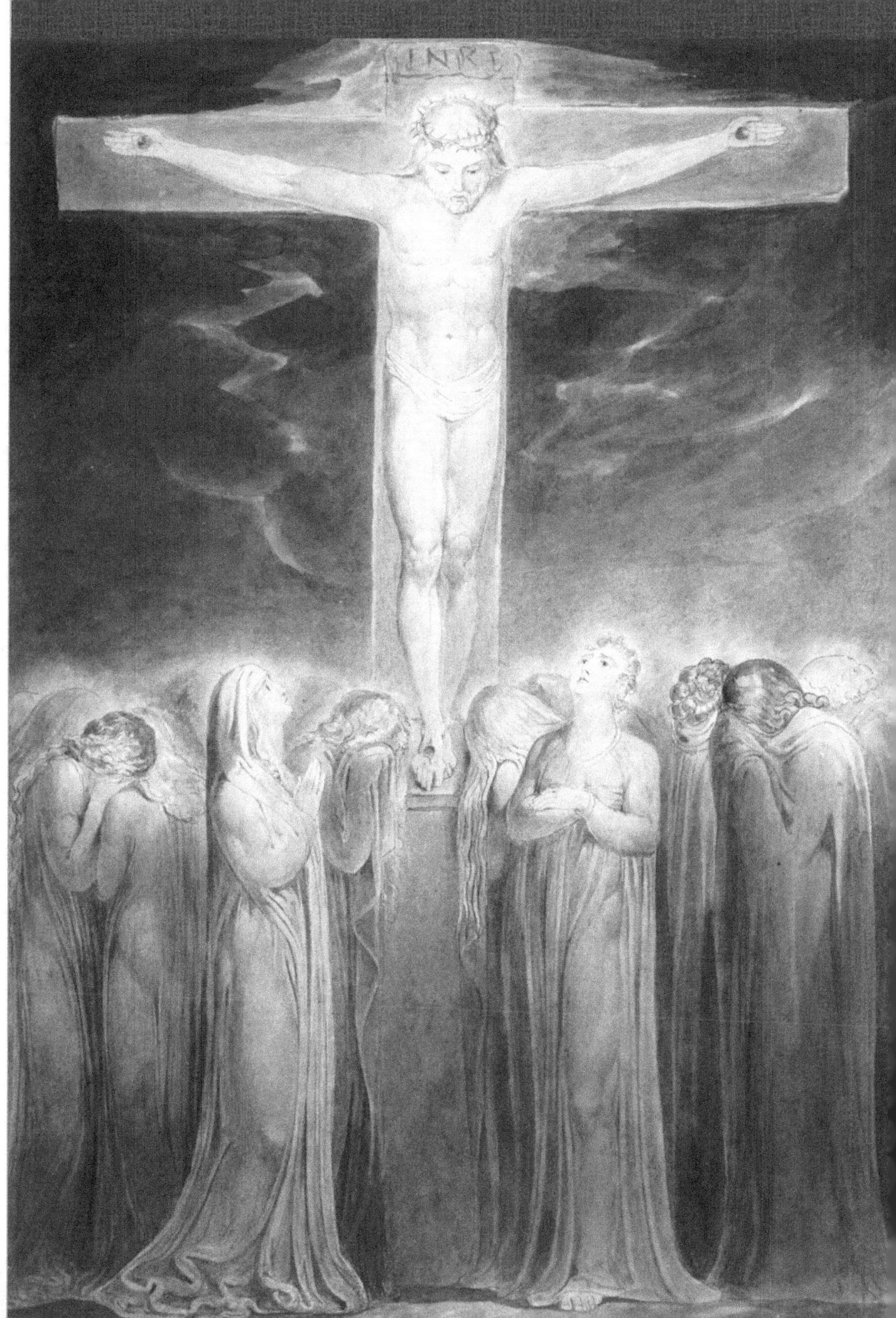

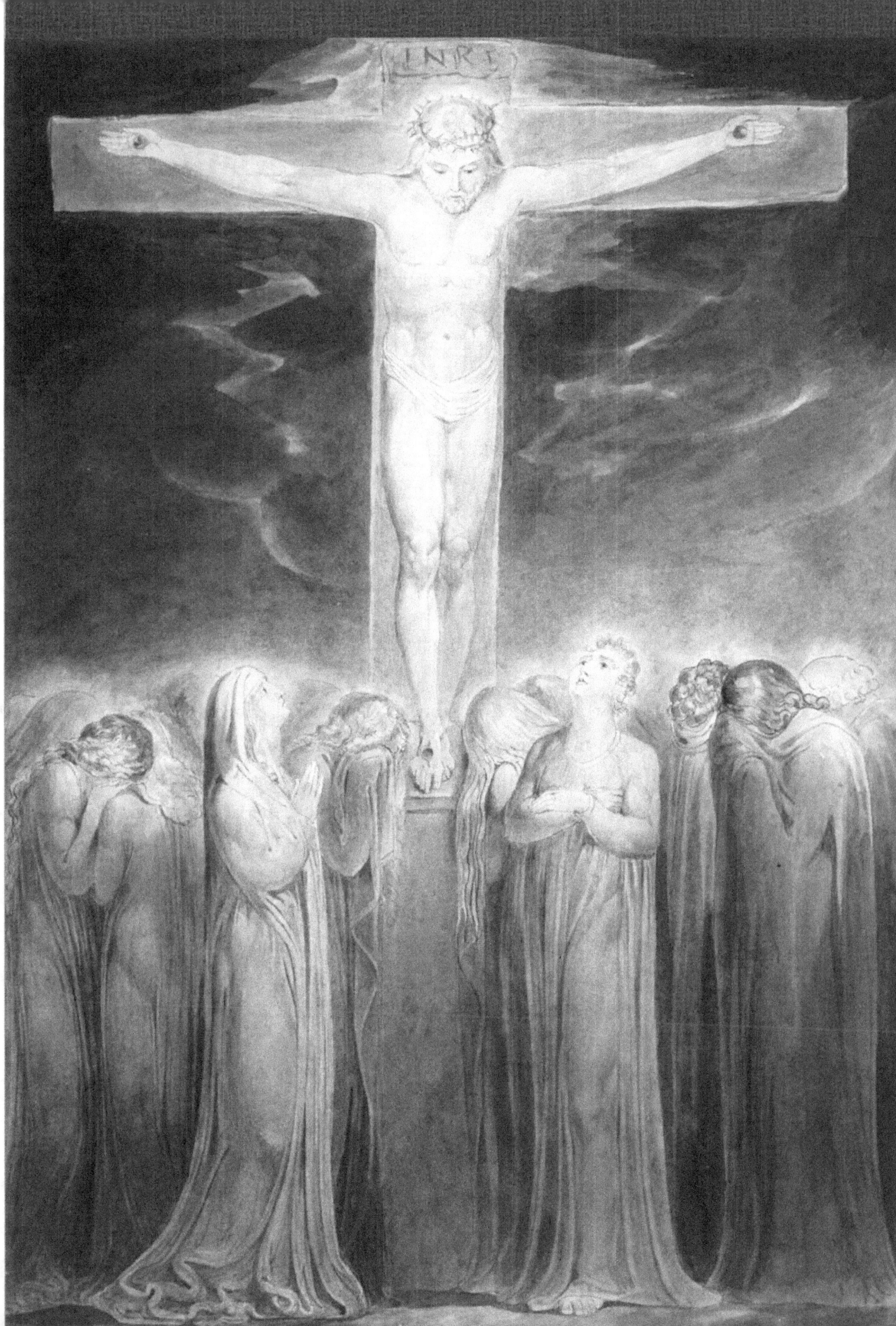

# THE BODY OF CHRIST BORNE TO THE TOMB

c. 1799-1800
Tempera on canvas backed by cardboard.
26.7 x 37.8 mm.
Location: Tate Britain.

Blake here combines the accounts of Christ's burial found in the four Gospels by including all of the characters mentioned in them:

Christ's dead body wrapped in linen.

Joseph of Arimathea, who provides the tomb.

Nicodemus, who brings a gift of aloe and myrrh for the ritual.

Mary, the mother of Jesus.

Mary Magdalene and another woman.

The young man at the fore is probably John, the Gospel author.

Usually, artists depict scenes of Christ's burial as dramatic and emotional—like most of Blake's art. So why is this image so linear and calm? Maybe it has to do with Blake's ideas of order and rationality—that Jesus's death fits into an orderly plan. Regardless, I bet he wants to make another point: one that contrasts the icky material world below (shown as overwhelmingly covered in hyper-vertical lines) with the heavenly, spiritual realm (shown as hyper-horizontal and above the rest). Jesus's dead body seems to float above the others, horizontal, flush with the horizontal lines of the sky. In this way, Blake might be saying that Jesus—especially in his death—connects the spiritual and material worlds.

Then again, this is Blake. He might be up to all kinds of mischief.

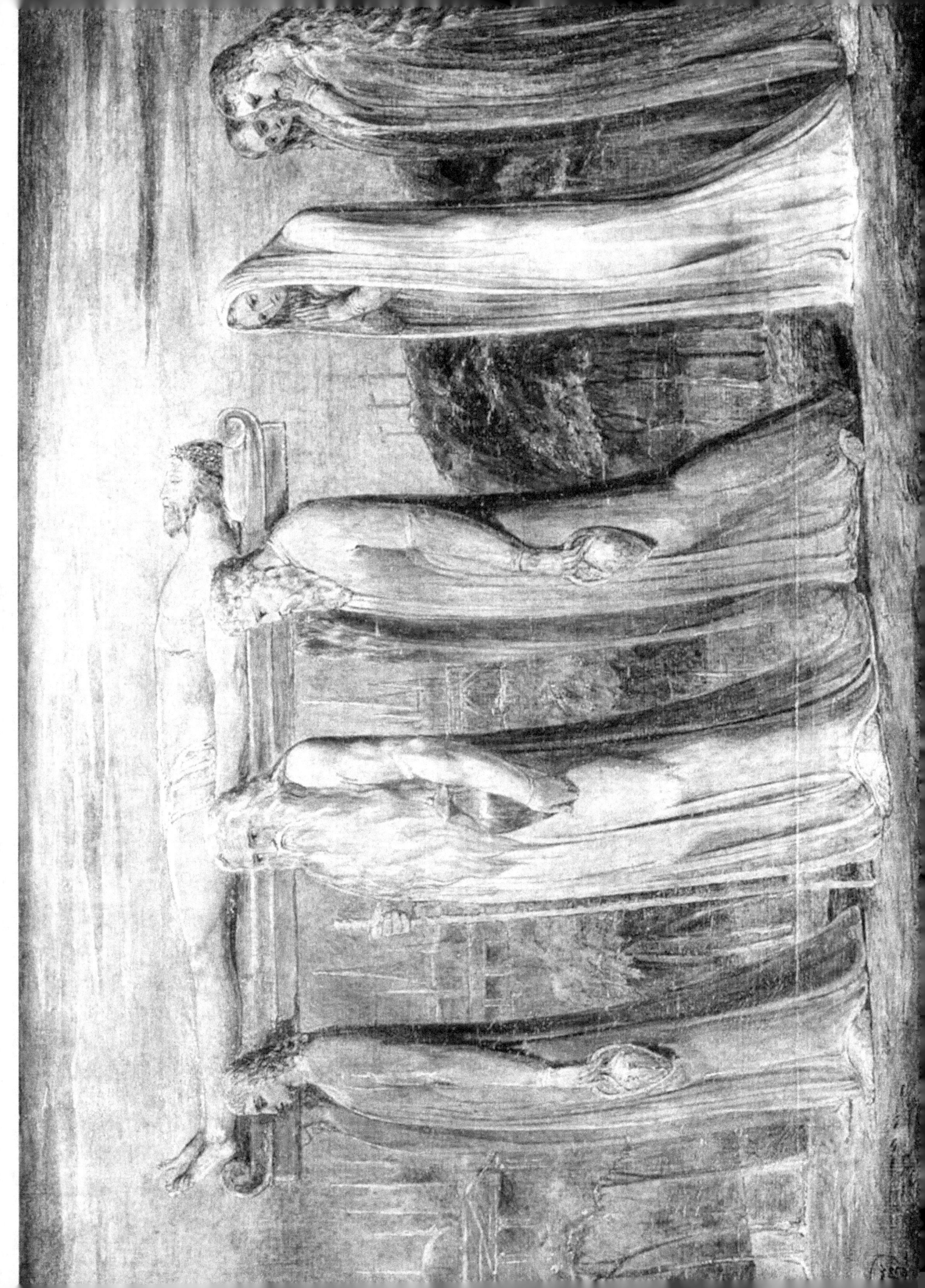

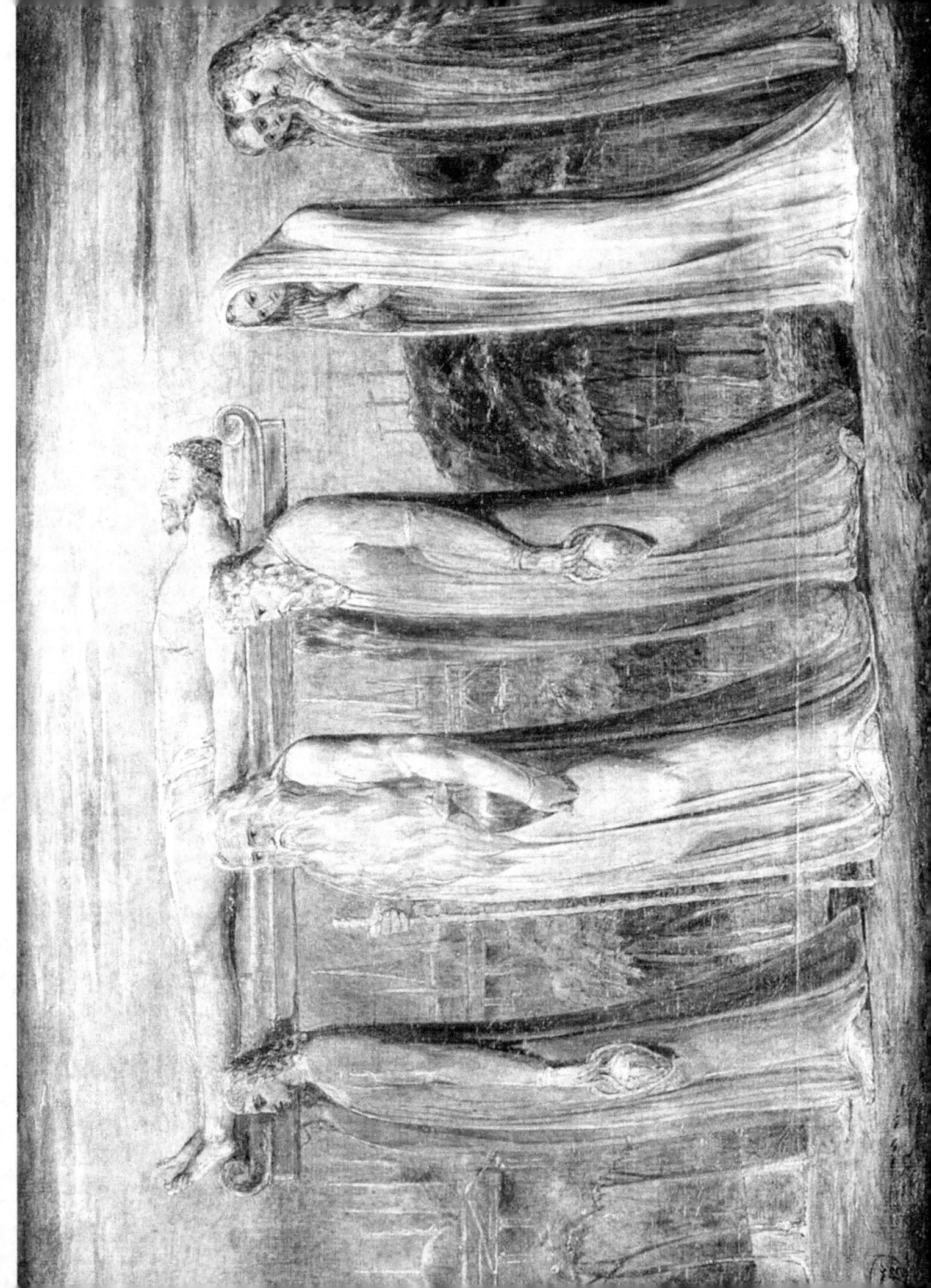

# PART 4

# OTHER CHRISTIAN THEMES

# ANGEL OF REVELATION

c. 1803-1805
Ink, pen, graphite, & watercolor.
39.2 x 26 cm.
Location: The Met.

Also titled, "And the angel which I saw lifted up his hand to Heaven."

Blake illustrates the Book of Revelation 10, where its author, John of Patmos, has a vision of a massive angel with a cloud for clothing, a rainbow on his head, a face like the sun, and pillars of fire for feet. The text in the angel's hand looks like both a Bible and popular portrayals of Moses's Ten Commandments on two stone tablets. The horsemen are the thunder, alluding to the horsemen of the apocalypse in that same book of the Bible. Plenty of earlier Christian art portrayed colossal angels, especially the Angel of Judgment. Many think the stance of the angel imitates drawings of the historic Colossus of Rhodes.

The angel stands on both land and sea—an echo of the duality of Blake's Behemoth and Leviathan. What does this represent for Blake? I don't really know, but I bet it's all kinds of stuff.

As a fellow mystic and seer of visions, Blake probably felt a deep kinship with the tiny man gazing up at the hulking angel.

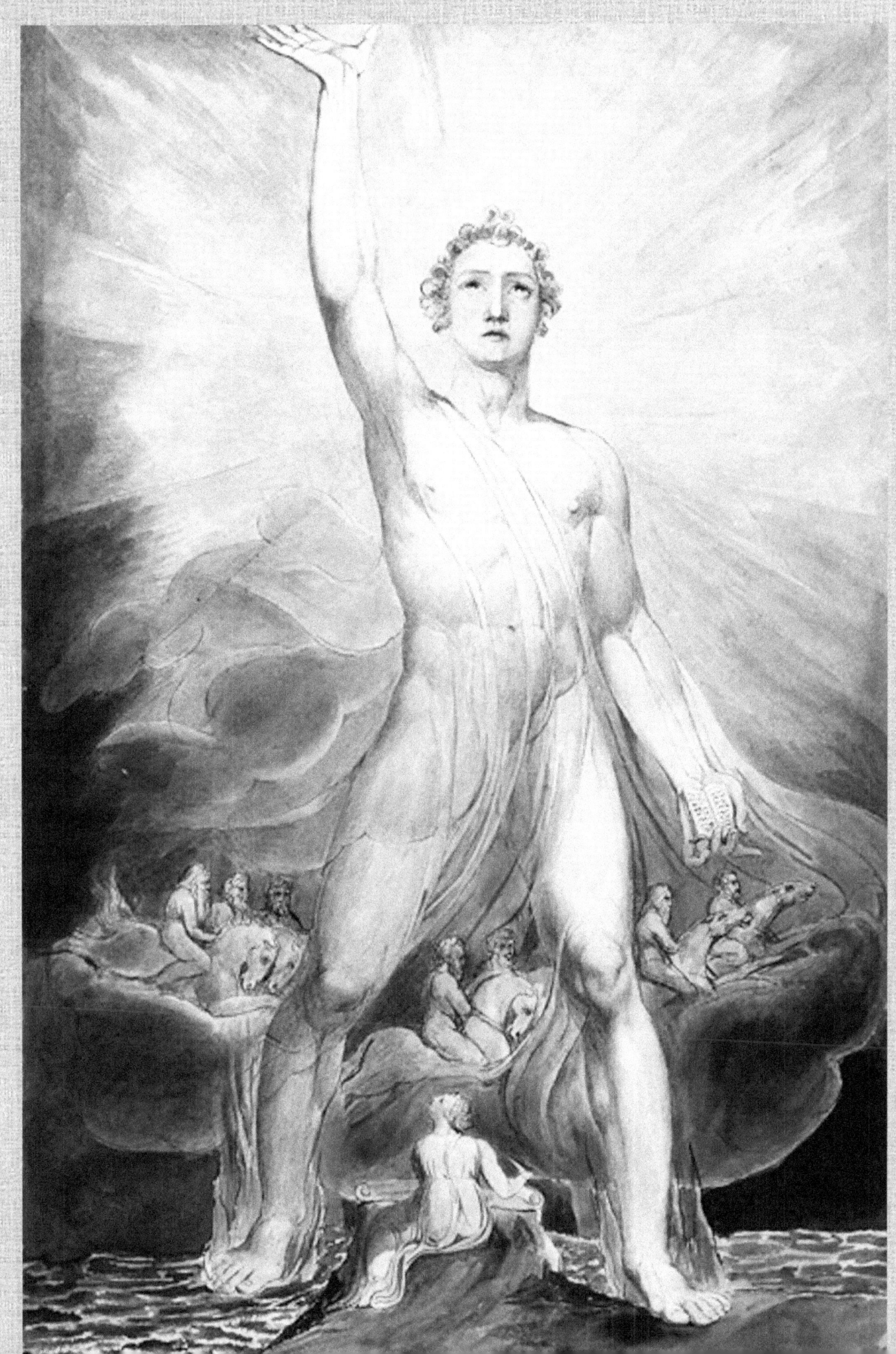

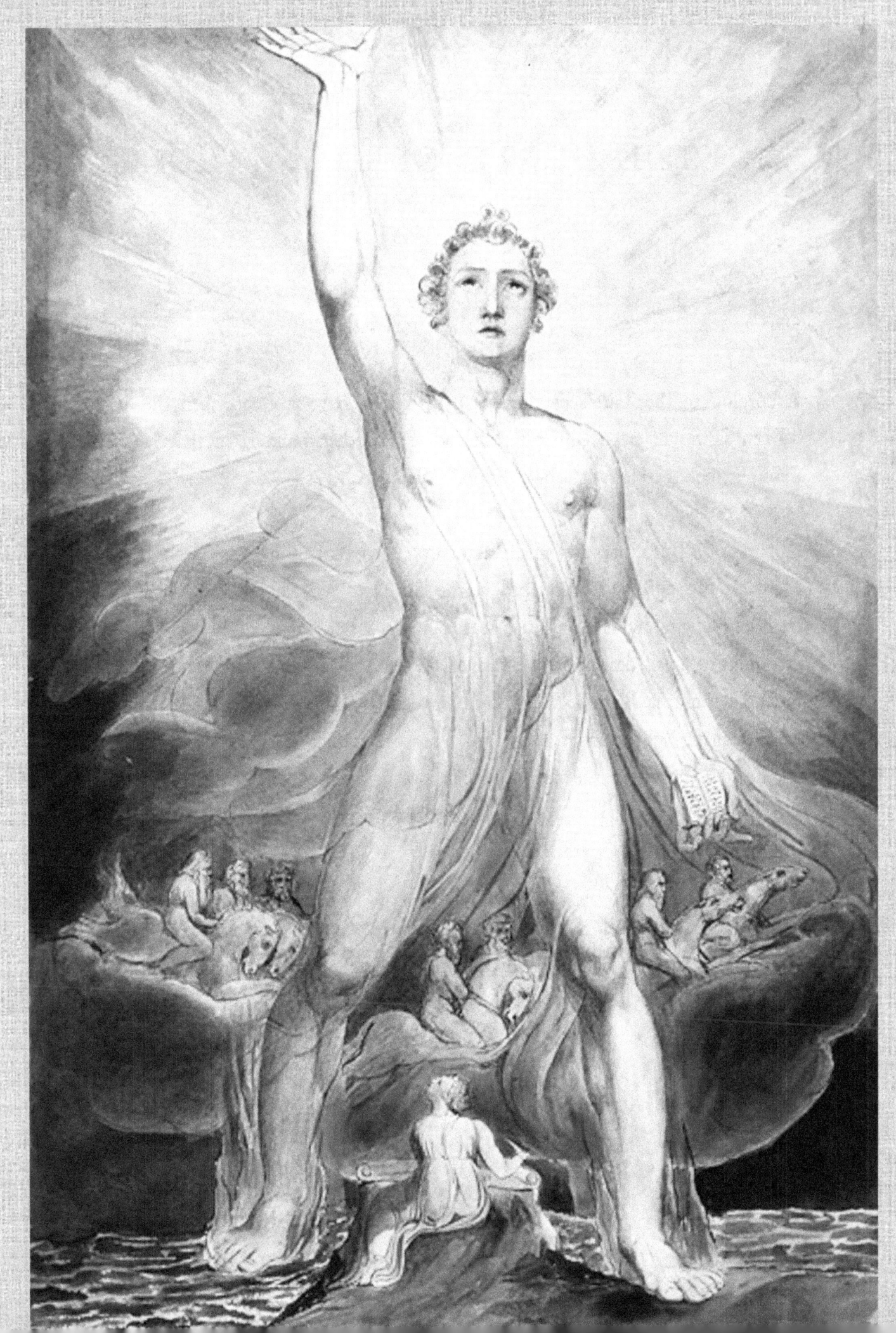

# THE DEATH OF THE VIRGIN

1803
Watercolor on paper.
37.8 x 37.1 cm.
Location: Tate Britain.

According to the Tate's catalogue entry, Blake may have inscribed this with "Then saith He to the disciple, 'Behold thy Mother!' and from that hour that Disciple took her unto his own home.' John, xix, 27."

Apparently, Byzantine and medieval artists liked portraying the death of the Virgin Mary. Although never described in the Bible, it became a common part of the tradition, imagining it as a holy death and ascension, and maybe even a way of imagining a good death for the rest of us, too. The long lines of the figures resemble those of Blake's "The Body of Christ Borne to the Tomb." Interestingly, light seems to flow from her chest—not just from Jesus or heaven— maybe a testament to the purity of her love or holiness of her heart. Jesus, angels, and little cherub thingies flying in a rainbow see the Mother of God through the transition.

Yet death is terrible, tho' borne on angels' wings.
—Blake's Poetical Sketches: King Edward the Third, line 497

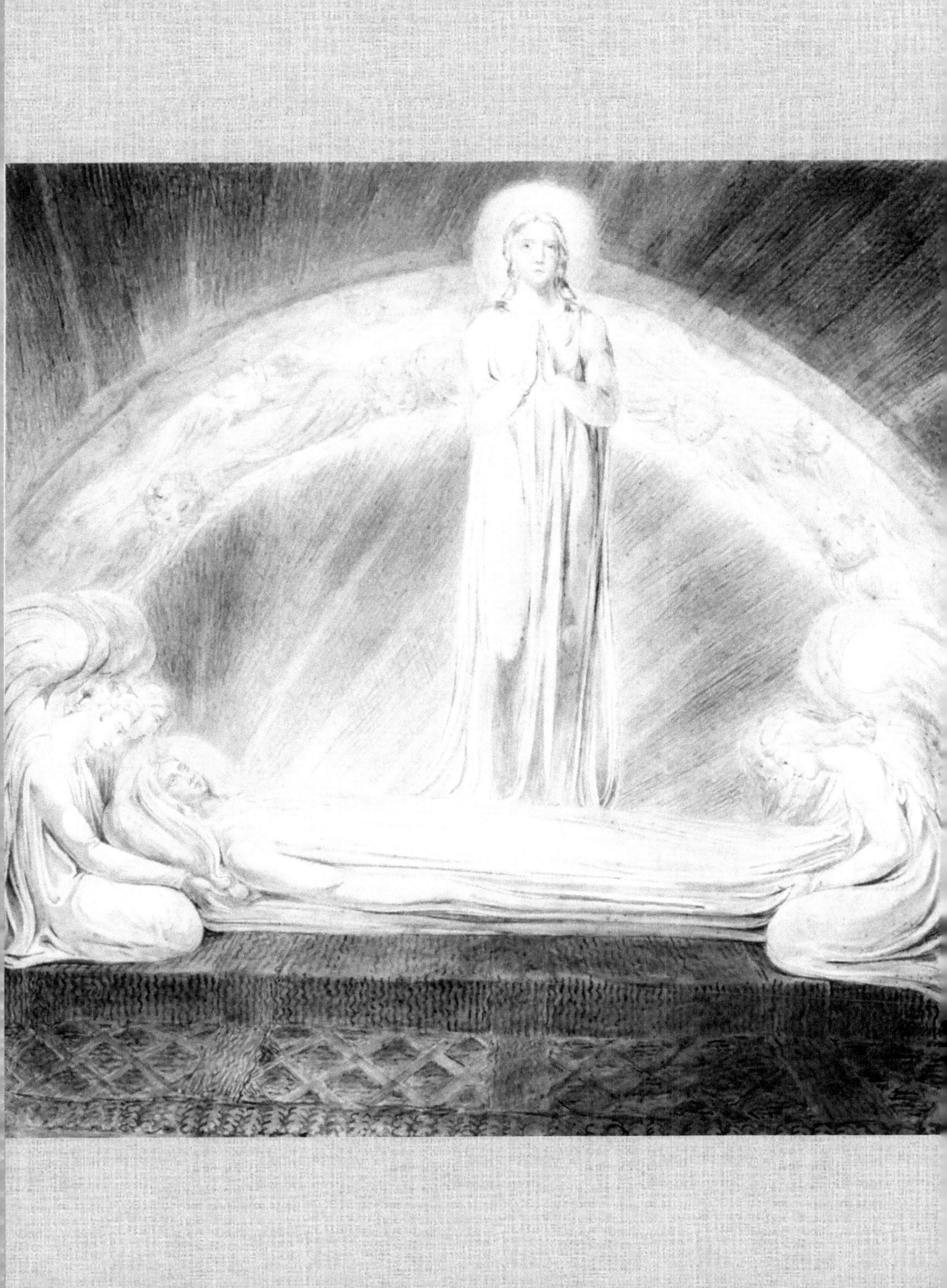

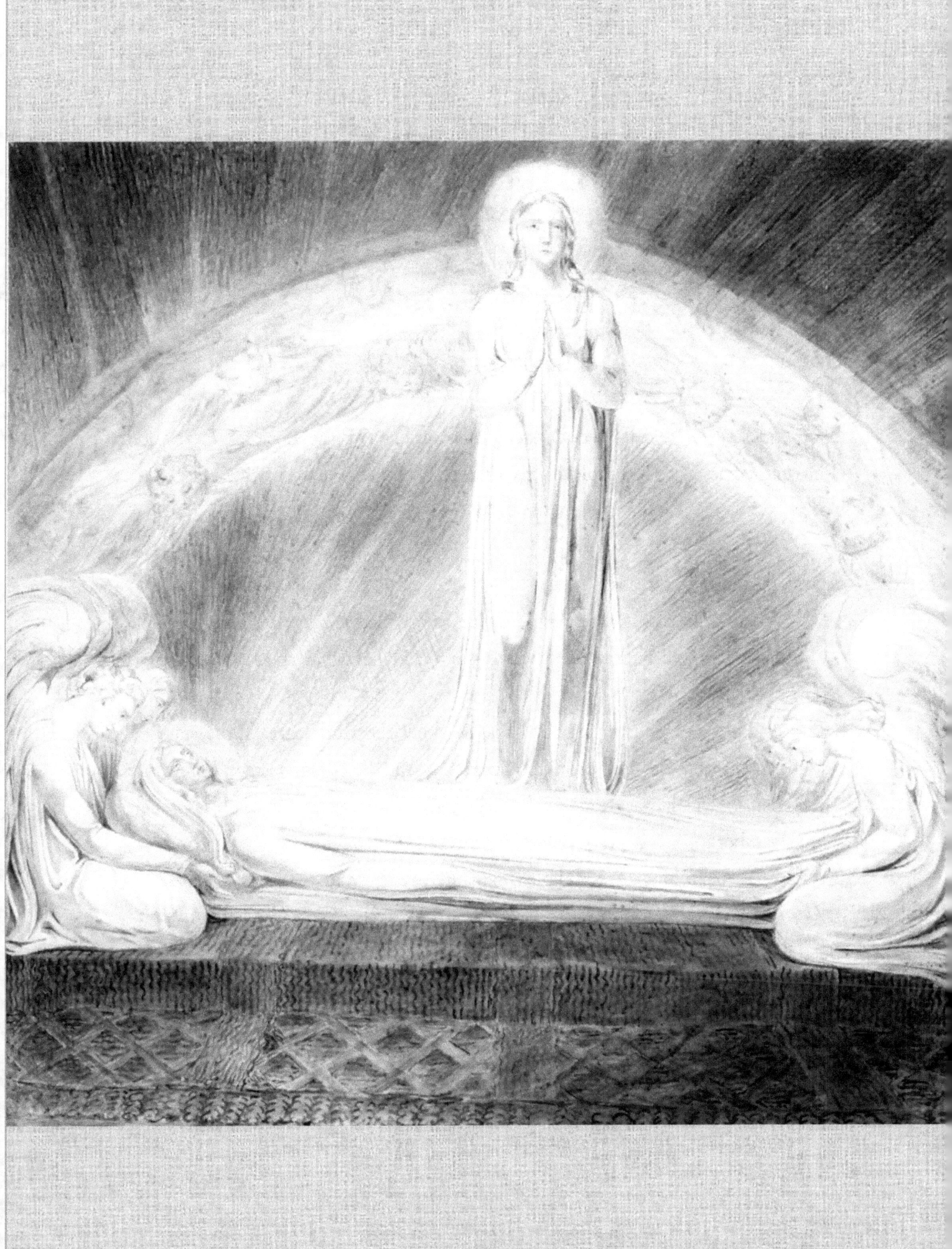

# THE RED DRAGON
# AND THE WOMAN
# CLOTHED WITH THE SUN

c. 1803-1805

43.7 x 34.8 cm.

Location: The Brooklyn Museum.

Blake did several "Great Red Dragon" illustrations for the Book of Revelation. This one comes with a couple of inscriptions that quote Revelations 12:1 and 12:4.

Above the image, it reads:

>Woman clothed with the sun, & the moon under her feet, and
>upon her head a crown of twelve stars; and behold a great red dragon also.

Below the image, it says:

>And the tail of the great red dragon drew the third part of the stars of heaven, and did cast them to the earth. And the dragon stood before the woman which was ready to be delivered for to devour her child as soon as it was born.

At least the next lines of Revelation explain that she and the child escape.

But seriously, Blake, you picked a passage that is 100% disturbing.

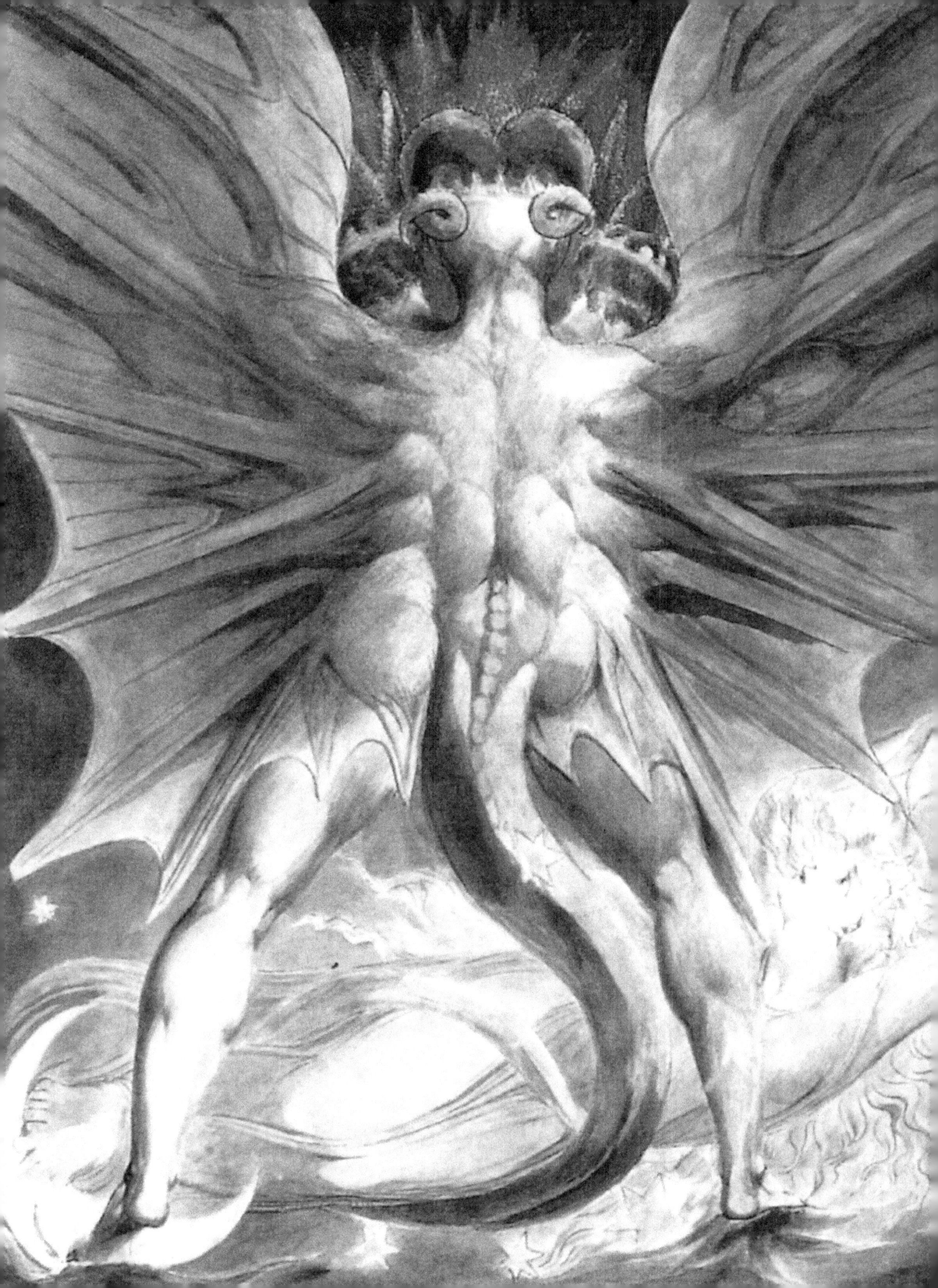

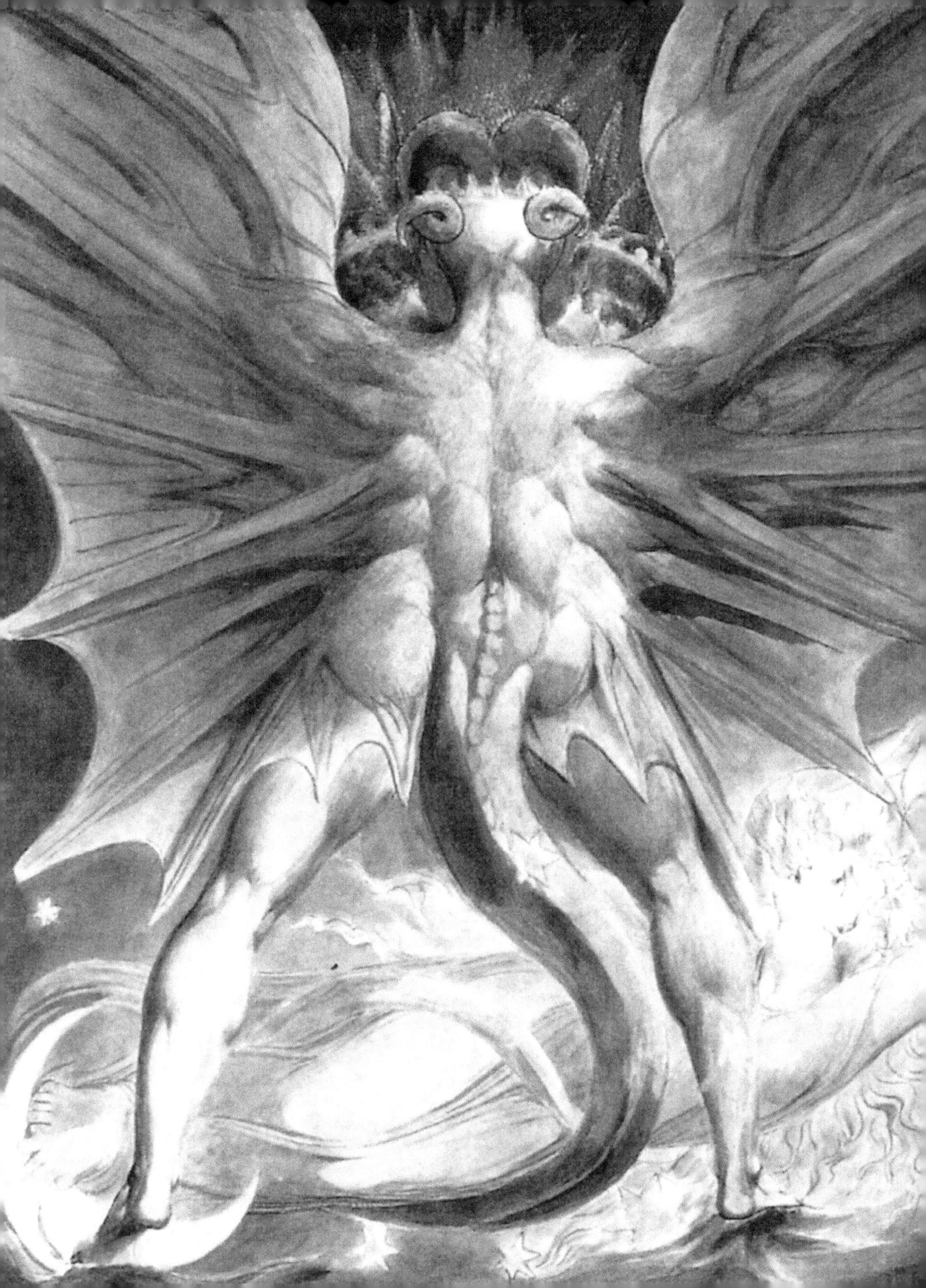

# PART 5

# DANTE THEMES

# CERBERUS
# (FROM DANTE'S DIVINE COMEDY)

1824-1827.

Graphite, ink, & watercolor on paper.

37.2 x 52.8 cm.

Location: Tate Britain.

Blake illustrated Dante's 3-part Divine Comedy, a massively influential medieval text about its author's imagined descent into a nine-leveled Hell (Inferno), passage through Purgatory (Purgatorio), and ascent into heavenly Paradise (Paradiso).

Cerberus isn't just a pet at Hogwarts. Dating back to Greek mythology, Cerberus is the hound of Hell, making sure dead folk don't leave. He got the reputation of being ravenous, so in Dante's Divine Comedy, Cerberus is a guard-dog for the circle of Hell reserved for gluttons. The fictive Dante's guide through Hell, Virgil, throws dirt into the dog's maws so they can escape.

In his Marriage of Heaven and Hell, Blake offers "Proverbs of Hell," including this one:

"The road of excess leads to the palace of wisdom."

So does gluttony lead to a palace of wisdom, or to a three-headed Hell hound?

Word on the street is that Blake once said, "Dante saw devils where I see none. I see only good." Well, Blake certainly wasn't in agreement with Dante on "Heaven" and "Hell" and all that, but I think Blake saw his fair share of devils...!

(Quote's source: Henry Crabb Robinson's Diary, Reminiscences and Correspondence.)

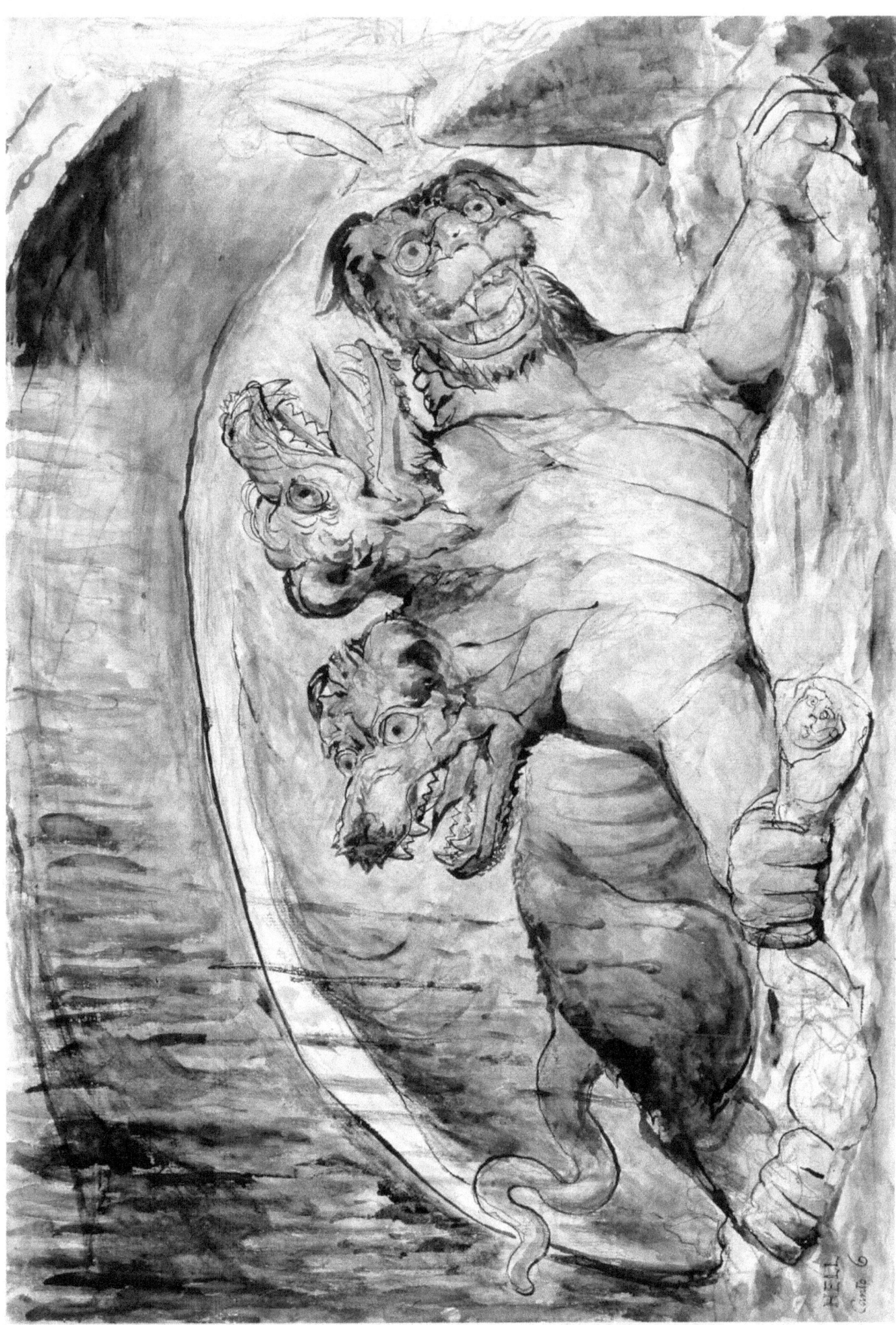

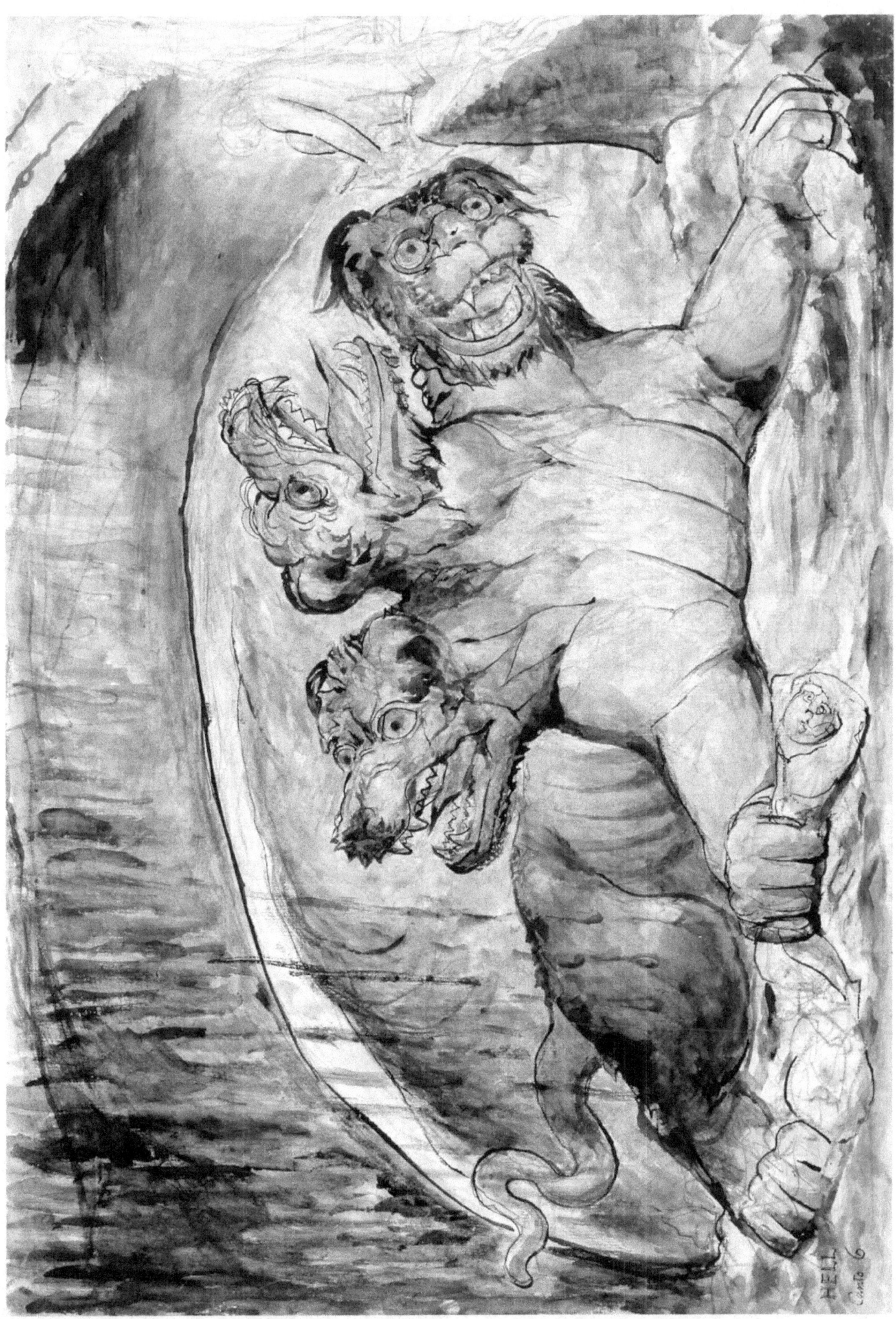

# THE DEVILS WITH DANTE AND VIRGIL BY THE POOL

1824-1827
Graphite, ink, & watercolor on paper.
37.2 x 52.7 cm.
Location: Tate Britain.

"What's that?  I don't know, but I like it!"

After learning what it's about, I'm on the fence.  When does creepiness go from cool to *oh-no-thank-you*?  I'll have to sit with that while I color this.

In this illustration from the Inferno, or the Hell part of Dante's Divine Comedy, we see Dante's eighth circle of Hell.  Dante and Virgil and their devil escorts look on while a group of corrupt officials drown in a pool of boiling pitch reserved just for them.

*Eeeek*.  Maybe we need one of those pools around here.  Or maybe it'd fill up too fast.

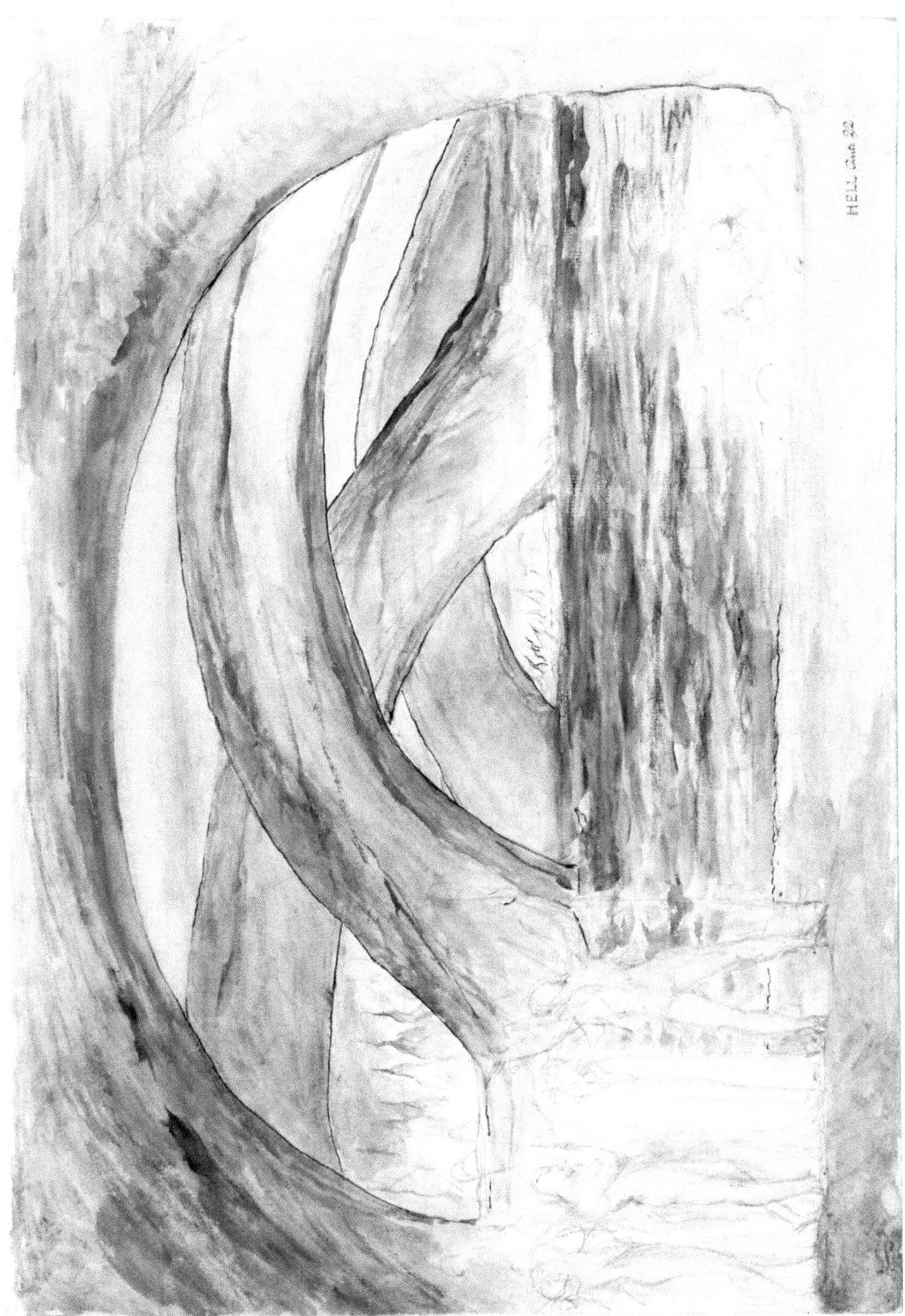

HELL Seite 22

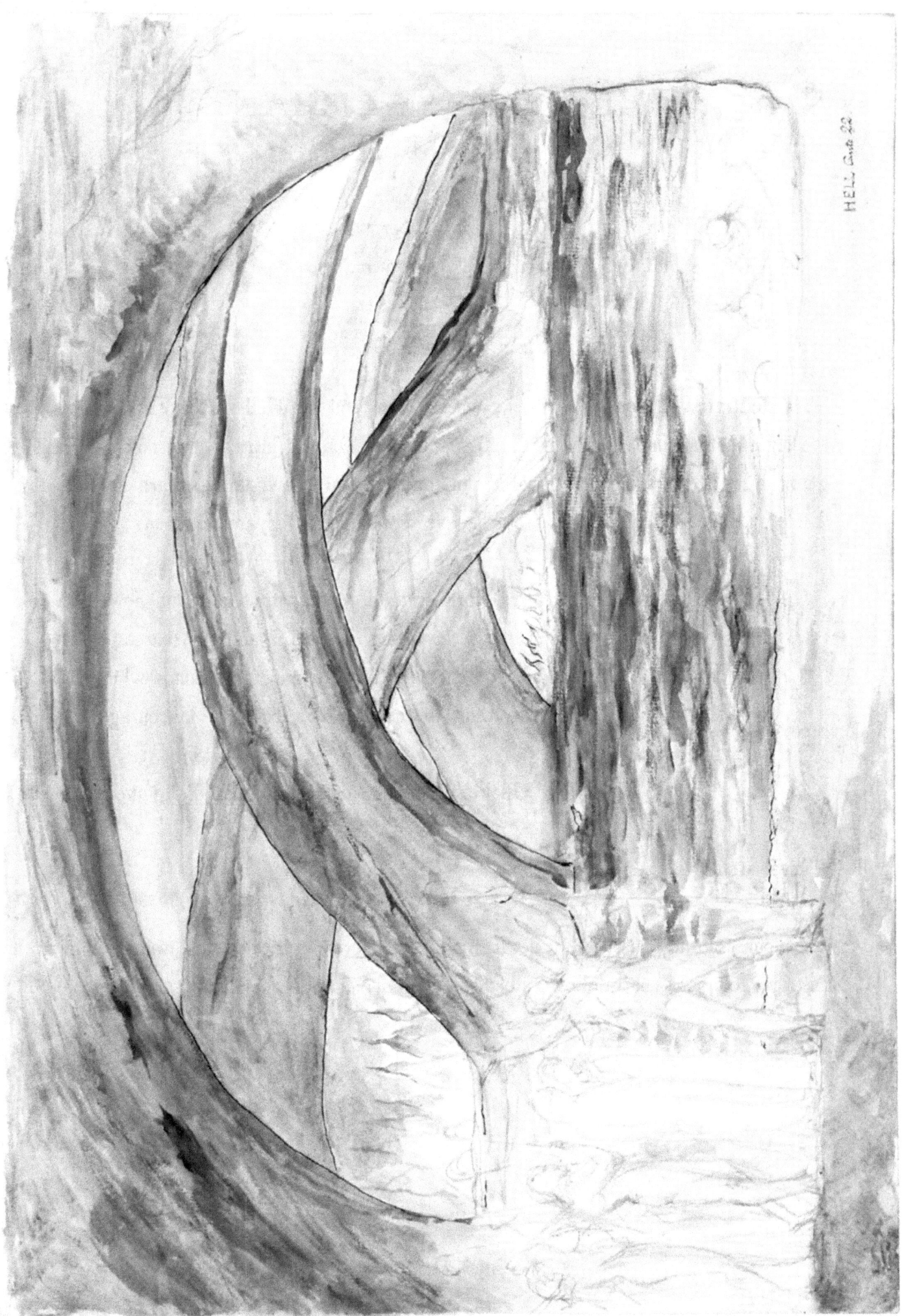

HELL Canto 22

# THE PRIMEVAL GIANTS
# SUNK IN THE SOIL

1824-1827
Graphite, ink, chalk, & watercolor on paper.
37.2 x 52.7 cm.
Location: Tate Britain.

This illustrates <u>Inferno</u> 31: 19-45, when Dante and his Hell-guide, Virgil, leave the eighth circle and see the primeval giants. In Blake's intricate mythology, these giants were creators of the sensual realm, and they are now sunk beneath the Sea of Time and Space, representatives of the five senses trapped by materialism.

The Giants who formed this world into its sensual existence, and now seem to live in it in chains, are in truth the causes of its life and the sources of all activity; but the chains are the cunning of weak and tame minds which have power to resist energy. According to the proverb, the weak in courage is strong in cunning.

~Blake's <u>Marriage of Heaven and Hell,</u> line 125.

I never would've guessed.

For your coloring purposes, you can make this picture whatever you want. Like the five colors of the rainbow embodied, or a nudist basketball team, enjoying a leisurely day at the beach.

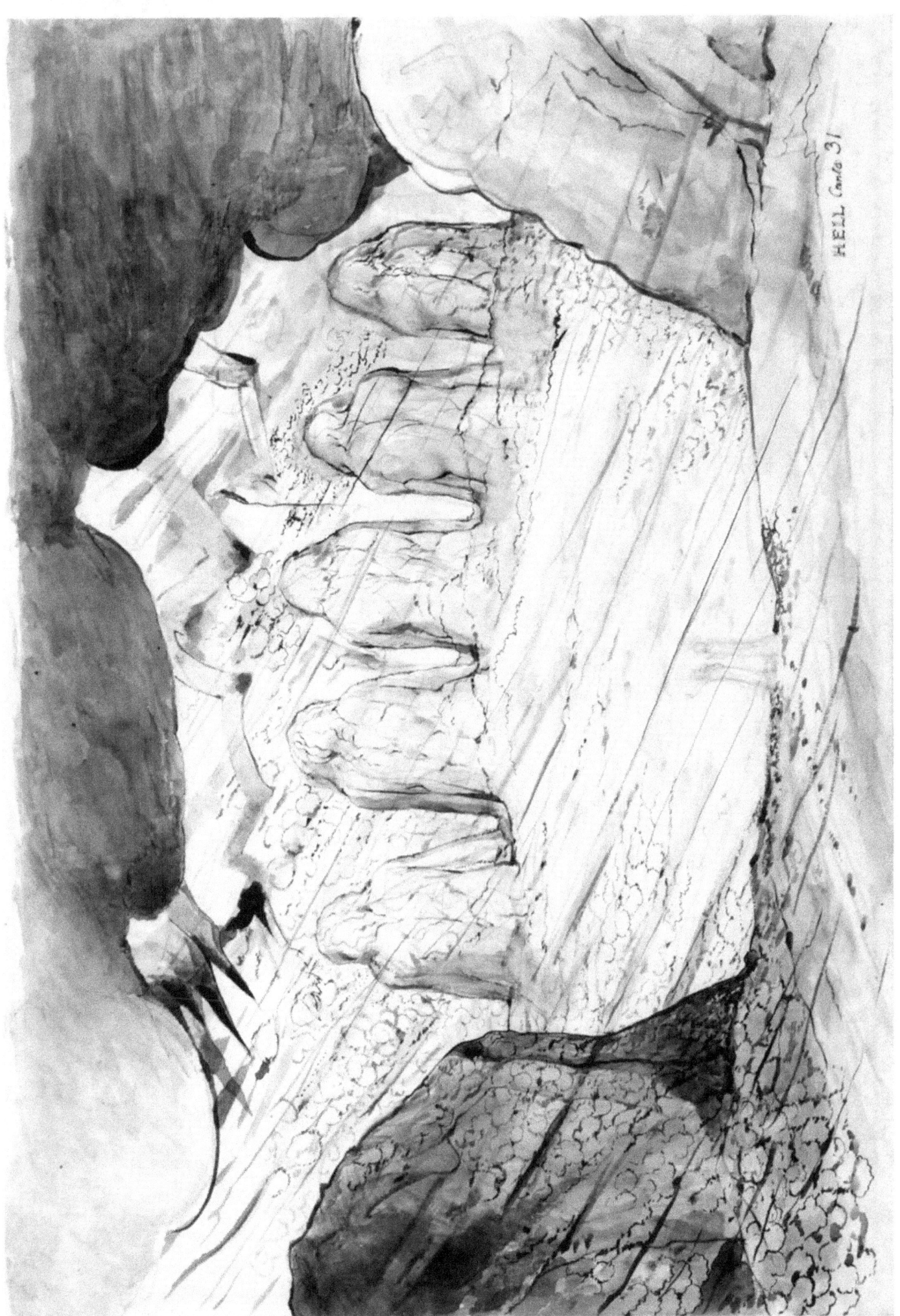

HELL Canto 31

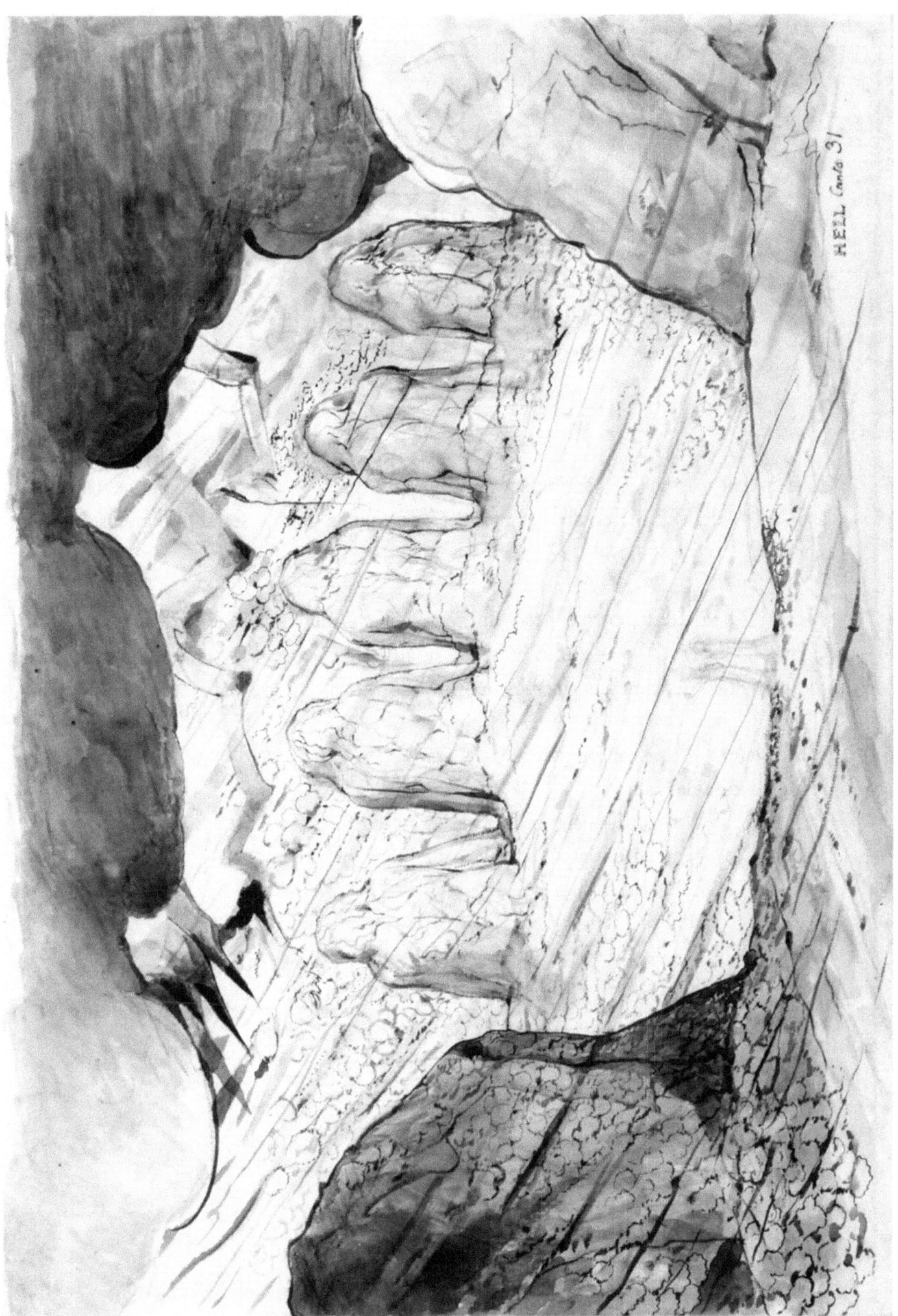

HELL Canto 31

# THE ASCENT OF
# THE MOUNTAIN OF PURGATORY

1824-1827
Graphite, ink, & watercolor on paper.
52.8 x 37.2 cm.
Location: Tate Britain.

The middle part of Dante's trilogy is about Purgatory. Here, the fictive Dante and his guide, Virgil, climb the Purgatory mountain to the Earthly Paradise on its summit.

Blake died in 1827, before he could complete his illustrations of *The* Divine Comedy, giving them an added sense of significance, especially since they're about the afterlife. Even when incomplete, the illustrations inspire imagination.

This picture illustrates Purgatorio's "Canto 4."
Here's a sample:

> We through the broken rock ascended, close
> Pent on each side, while underneath the ground
> Ask'd help of hands and feet. When we arriv'd
> Near on the highest ridge of the steep bank,
> Where the plain level open'd I exclaim'd,
> "O master! I say which way can we proceed?"

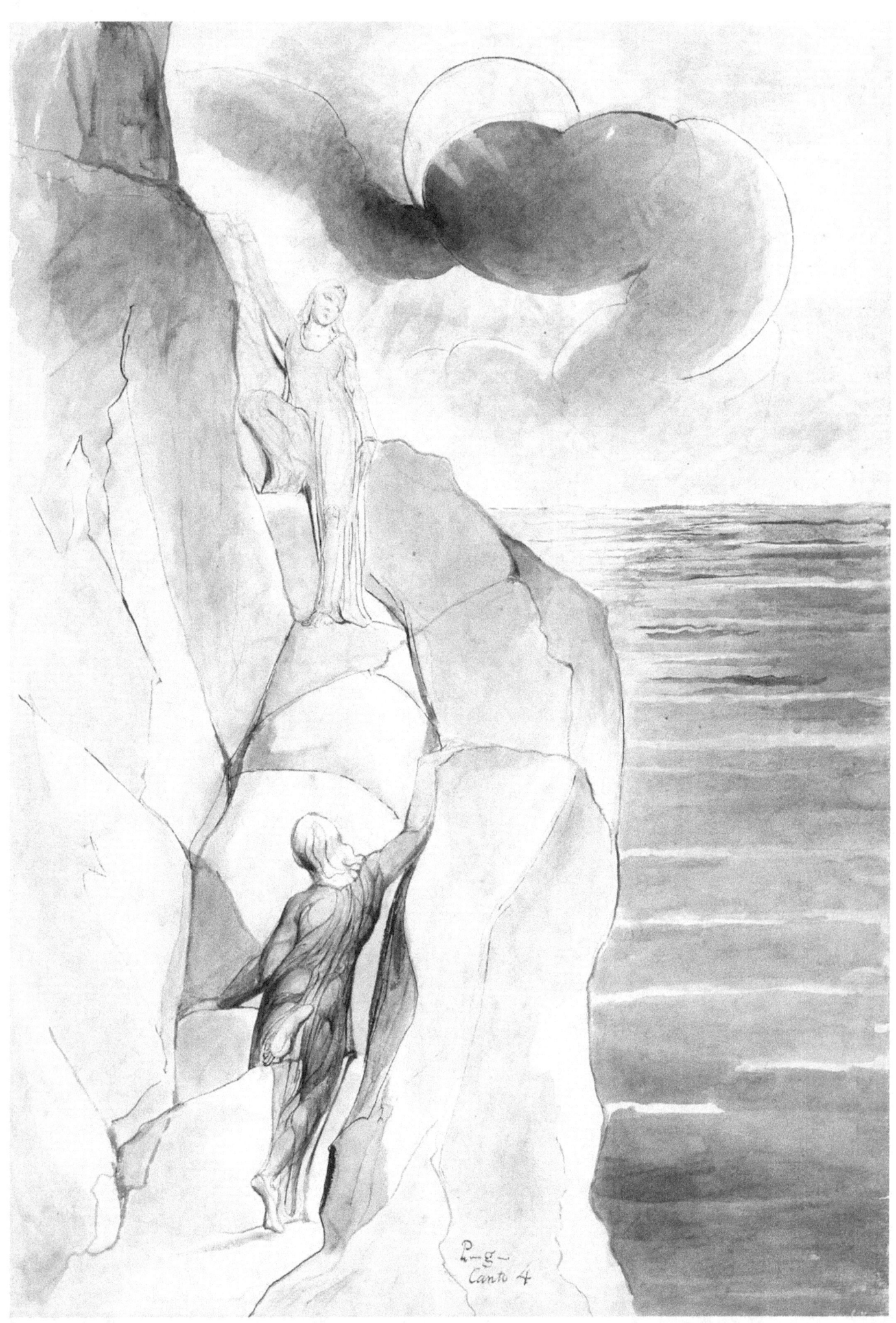

P—g—
Canto 4

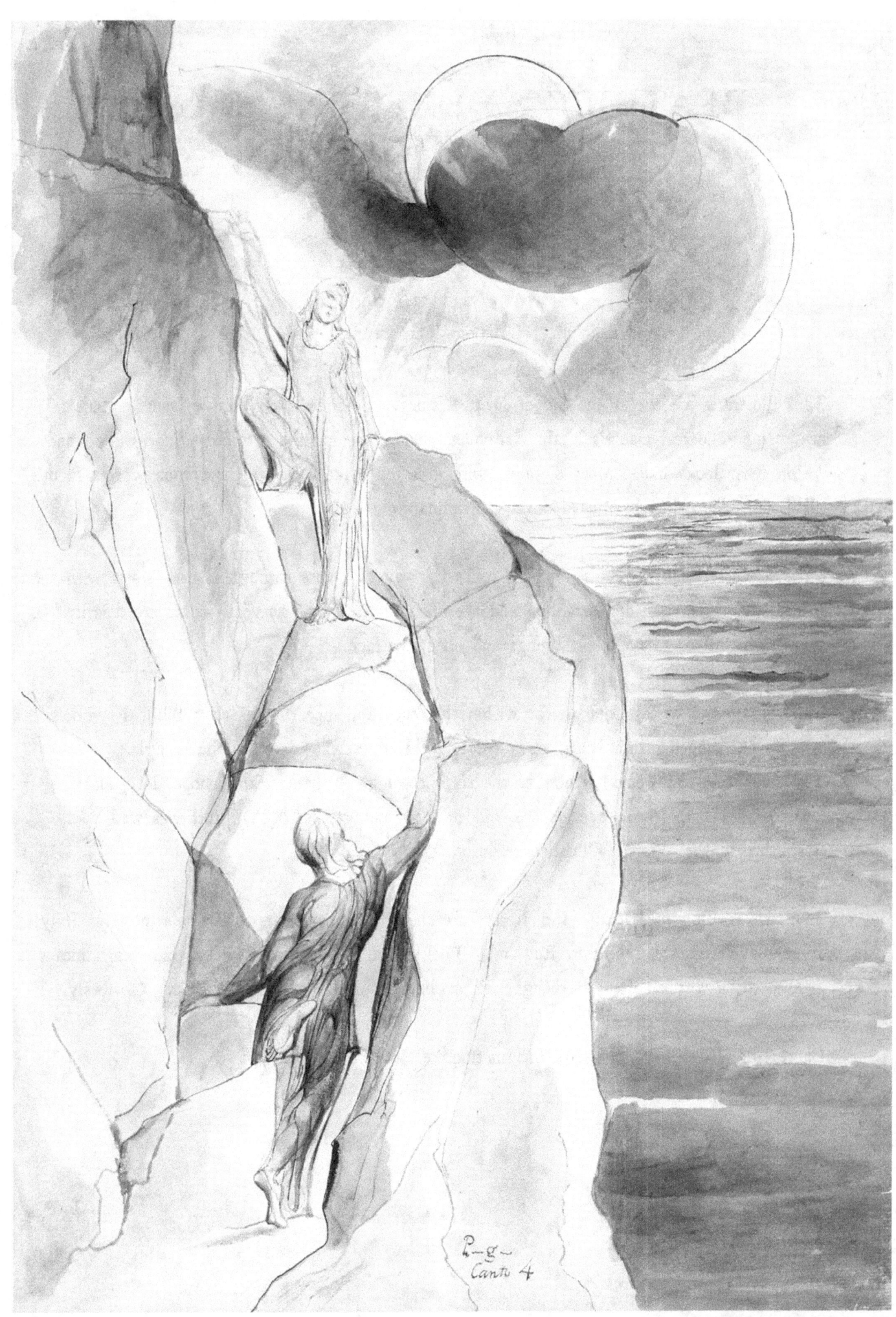

P—g—
Canto 4

# BEATRICE ADDRESSING DANTE FROM THE CAR

1824-1827
Ink & watercolor on paper.
37.2 x 52.7 cm.
Location: Tate Britain.

This illustrates a scene at the end of Dante's story. Beatrice is the fictive Dante's guide in heaven (and the real Dante's idealized woman). Here she looks a lot like Christ. She stands within what looks like octopus tentacles with eyes for suckers, above the octopus vortex mouth filled with ghost cherubs sucked down the drain.

More seriously, this weirdness—coming to us by way of Dante through Blake—starts with the Bible, where cherubim and seraphim and the creatures of God's heavenly court are described as having eyes all over and special wings and changing faces.

The four gospel writers' heads float within the tentacles, appearing as their biblical symbols. (Matthew = winged man. Mark = winged lion. Luke = winged ox. John = eagle.)
The two groups of women symbolize the three theological virtues (faith, hope, love) and the four cardinal virtues (prudence, justice, moderation, courage). All that stuff was well-established in the Western Christian tradition.

The title is a bit misleading—I'm pretty sure they didn't have cars in Dante's medieval Italy, or in Blake's nineteenth-century England. Looking at the picture, it seems that "car" means giant octopus vortex. Really, though, it's a chariot pulled by a giant griffin. Obviously.

Dante, like Blake, had an active imagination.

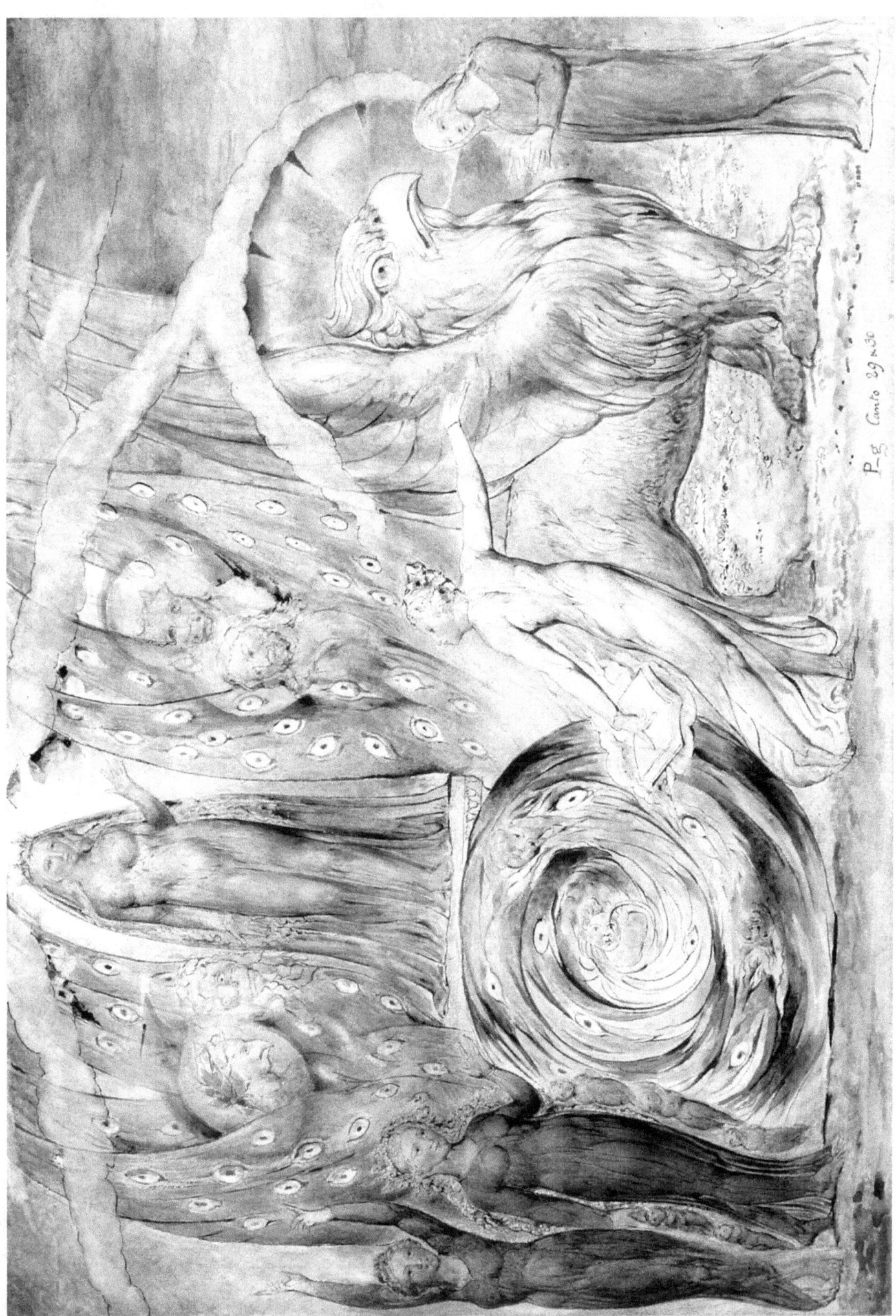

P. g   Canto 29.30

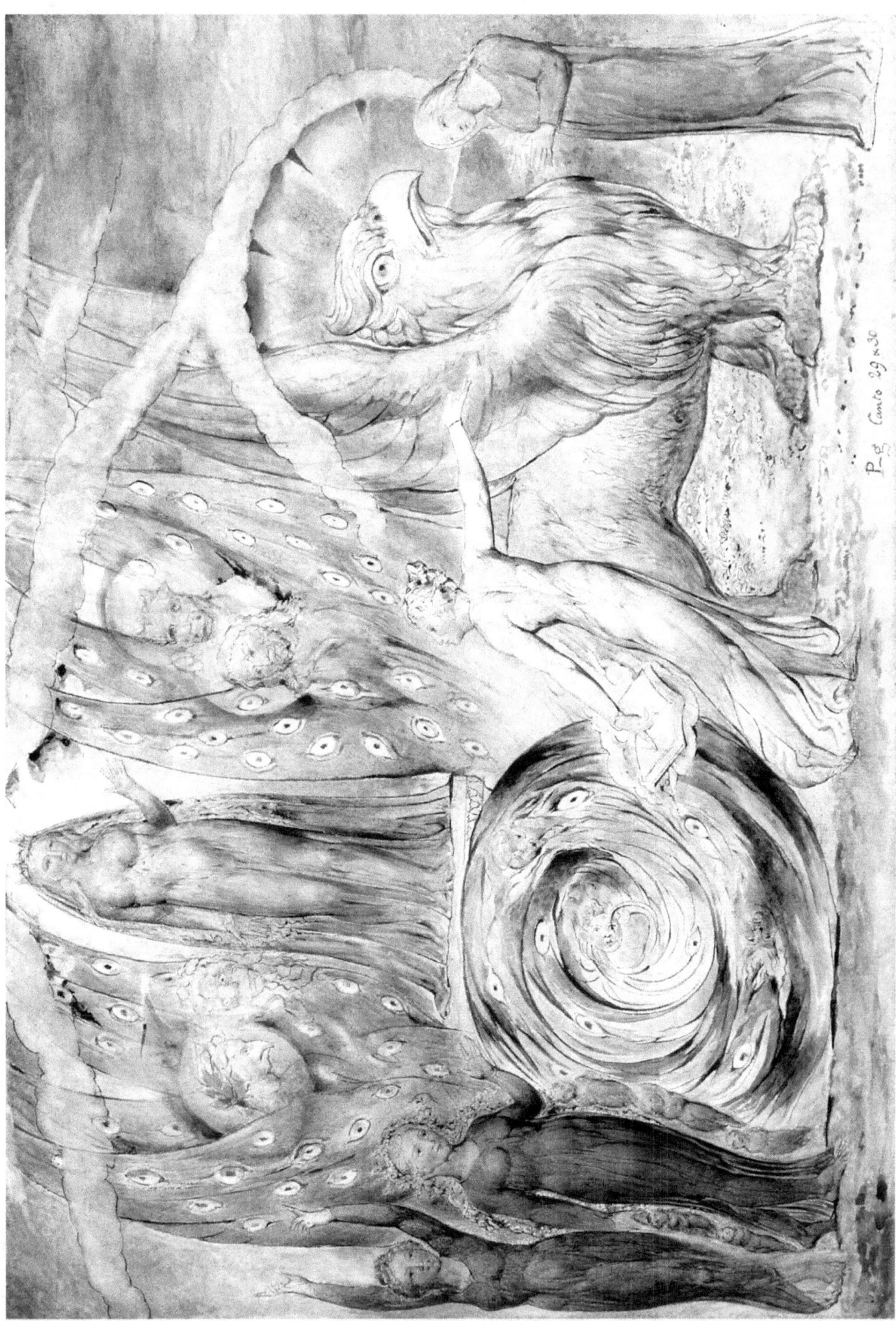

P. Canto 29-30

# A note from the artist

Dear colorist:

Thank you for using my coloring book—I hope it helped your imagination soar!

I love hearing from you and seeing your artwork, and I also need Amazon reviews to keep this eccentric Blake book going.  If this coloring book served any good purpose, I'd be grateful for your review.

## To submit a review if you purchased the book:

- sign in to your Amazon account
- click on "Orders"
- find the product listing among your Orders
- click "Write a product review" on the right

## To submit a review no matter how you got the book:

- find our product page (for example, by searching "Color Me Blake Adult Coloring Book")
- scroll down to the reviews section
- click "Write a customer review," located to the right of the star-rating breakdown

Thanks 😊
Jacki Price